CALKE ABBEY

DERBYSHIRE

A Hidden House Revealed

THE NATIONAL TRUST

CALKE ABBEY

DERBYSHIRE

A Hidden House Revealed

Howard Colvin

The National Trust/George Philip

1985

British Library Cataloguing in Publication Data

Colvin, H. M.
    Calke Abbey.
    1. Calke Abbey – History   2. Calke (Derbyshire)
    – Monasteries – History
    I. Title
    942.5'19   DA690.C15/

    ISBN 0–540–01084–7

© This edition:
Antler Books Ltd 1985
11 Rathbone Place, London W1

All the pictures in this book were taken by Michael Freeman
except those supplied by the following:

Bodleian Library (H26Jur) 102r; *Howard Colvin* 9t, 11, 12b, 44, 49, 53, 60, 67, 70, 71, 74, 77, 104, 106, 107t & b, 110, 118, 121, 122, 123, 126; *Country Life* 51, 52; *National Monuments Record* 25; *National Trust* 37, 45, 75, 76; *Edward Piper* 29; *Lord Rossmore* 102l; *Yale Center for British Art* 103

Maps and diagrams by MJL Cartographics

Designed by Norman Turpin

Published by George Philip, 12–14 Long Acre, London WC2E 9LP,
in association with The National Trust

Reprinted 1986

Typesetting by Fakenham Photosetting Ltd
Originated and printed in Hong Kong by Mandarin Offset Ltd

Frontispiece: The south front of Calke Abbey.

CONTENTS

	Preface	7
1	Calke before the Harpurs	13
	Calke Priory	
	After the Dissolution	
2	The Rise of a Gentry Family	21
	The Founders of the Family	
	The First Three Baronets	
	Into the Aristocracy	
3	The World of the Harpur Crewes	48
	The Isolated Baronet	
	Sir George Crewe	
	The Last Two Baronets	
4	Calke Goes Public	77
5	The Estate	86
6	The House and its Contents	98
	The House	
	The Contents	
7	The Park and Gardens	118
	Index	127

PREFACE

ENGLISH HISTORY is to a very large extent the history of a landed aristocracy. From 1066, when the country was partitioned out among the victorious Norman barons, to the First World War, in which so many sons of the gentry perished, there are few aspects of English history in which the landed aristocracy did not, for better or for worse, play a leading part. Unlike the aristocracies of some other European countries, it never held itself aloof from the changing realities of contemporary life. This flexibility and adaptability enabled it to survive – and indeed to profit by – many social, political and economic mutations. But in the end English society changed so fundamentally that in the course of the last hundred years the landed aristocracy has lost its dominant role, leaving its members as the holders of hereditary titles that no longer carry with them the deference once accorded to superior rank, and as the owners of great country houses that have lost their function as the local centres of social, political and administrative activity. In an egalitarian society the titles persist merely as personal adornments, and such of the houses as survive do so mostly as historical and architectural monuments open to the public.

Calke Abbey is one of these relics of the aristocratic past, saved from the dissolution of the estate which once supported it to become a property of The National Trust. Its story is in many ways a typical one that could be told of many other English country houses. What makes Calke unique is the way its contents have survived largely undisturbed since the third quarter of the nineteenth century. Like a sealed archaeological deposit they give an authentic picture of a vanished society through its material possessions, not only pictures, furniture and works of art, but household goods and objects of everyday use. Like the Welsh Erddig or the Scottish Manderston, Calke is above all a social exhibit, where we can see with our own eyes the aristocratic world that we have lost as surely as we have lost the world of peasant farming that once supported it. But at Calke not only have the objects survived, but the documents that tell us about them and their owners: deeds,

The bedroom occupied by Sir Vauncey Harpur Crewe as a young man, photographed in a state of picturesque disorder in 1984.

7

accounts, marriage settlements, wills, inventories, diaries and letters. It is from these documents that we can reconstruct the lives of those who lived at Calke, and it is only by doing so that we can understand what we see in the house today. For Calke is a direct expression of its owners' fortunes and interests. But for the acquisitive acumen of a Tudor lawyer the name of Harpur would never have been heard of in Derbyshire. But for a long minority the great house would never have been built in its present form. And but for that hereditary aversion to society which for two centuries afflicted the Harpur-Crewe family, Calke today would be just one more country house in which the past has been tastefully adapted to the needs of modern life. It is therefore to the history of a wealthy and latterly a decidedly eccentric family that much of this book is devoted.

The circumstances in which this most private of houses became public property are described below (see p. 77). For the author the transfer of ownership to the National Trust in February 1985 meant the end of four years during which he had the privilege of being the first historian to explore the silent and secretive world of Calke Abbey, to read its archives and to discover its hidden treasures. That was a fascinating experience that cannot be repeated. There are, I hope, no more manuscripts rotting in damp deed-boxes, no more diamonds lying forgotten among old Christmas cards, no more chests full of eighteenth-century embroidered silk hidden in places so remote that even professional valuers had over-looked them. All in due course will be listed, classified and con-served by The National Trust. Something of the atmosphere of hereditary eccentricity which so strongly pervaded Calke in 1981 may inevitably be lost in the process. But as a result the house and its contents will be preserved for the enjoyment of all who care for historic buildings. It is primarily for their benefit that this book has been written. But I hope that this short account of Calke and its owners, based largely on documents hitherto inaccessible and not yet fully catalogued, will also be of some interest to local historians and even perhaps to those for whom the aristocracy and the landed estate are matters of scholarly concern. It is, of course, far from being a definitive account of either house, family or estate, and will certainly need to be modified as a result of further research.

If Rupert Gunnis were still alive, this book would have been dedicated to him. For it was in his genial company that in 1964 I first visited Calke. We went there at the invitation of his distant relation, Mr. Henry Jenney (now Mr. Henry Harpur-Crewe), temporarily in charge of the house at a time when its owner, his brother, was ill. It was a tantalising glimpse of a forbidden mansion whose inner recesses I was, with Mr. Harpur-Crewe's encouragement, to penetrate when he succeeded to the estate in 1981. But for his kindness in giving me the freedom of Calke and its archives, scarcely a word of this book could have been written.

To Miss Joan Sinar, the County Archivist of Derby-shire, I am indebted not only for her cooperation in rescuing the Harpur-Crewe family archives, but also for much subsequent help in using and interpreting them. Mr. L. C. J. Cox, Mr. Roger Pegg,

The Drawing Room in 1886 (top)
and 1984. Virtually everything that is
now in the room was there in 1886
and the general arrangement of the
furniture dates from the 1860s.

Mr. Christopher Preston, Miss Claudia Severn and Mr. Alfred Winfield have been kind enough to tell me much about the recent history of Calke that no document would ever have revealed. For help with specific architectural or historical problems I am grateful to Sir John Summerson, the Master of St. Peter's College, Oxford, Mr. Arthur Alexander, Mr. Maxwell Craven, Dr. Ivan Hall, Mr. Patrick King, Mr. Rodney Melville, Mr. M. A. Pearman and Mr. Edward Saunders. My wife has, as usual, been a shrewd and percipient critic of my text.

Oxford   *H.M.C.*

The Library in 1886 (below) and 1984. In the course of a hundred years there has been very little change in books, furniture or ornaments.

The Saloon in 1984, unchanged since 1886 (below), apart from the recent removal of the cases of stuffed birds on the right.

1 CALKE BEFORE THE HARPURS

Calke Priory

CALKE ABBEY, as its name suggests, was once a religious community: not in fact an abbey (a name given to the present mansion only in 1808), but a priory. The distinction was not important, but in principle, though by no means always in practice, the status of an abbey (headed by an abbot) was superior to that of a priory (headed by a prior). Those who lived and worshipped at Calke Priory were known as Austin canons because they followed the Rule of St. Augustine. This was a code of religious conduct attributed to St. Augustine, a North African bishop in the later days of the Roman Empire, and was designed for clergy who wished to live a common life like monks. Monks in those days were often laymen, but Austin canons were always priests. In England and Wales there were some two hundred Augustinian abbeys and priories, of which the best-known included Christchurch in Hampshire, Dunstable in Bedfordshire, Waltham in Essex, St. Frideswide's in Oxford, and St. Bartholomew's in Smithfield, London. In Derbyshire there were Augustinian houses at Breadsall, Darley and Church Gresley and there was another almost within sight of Calke at Breedon-on-the-Hill in Leicestershire.

Nearly all these monasteries were founded in the twelfth century, a period when social and religious pressures combined to induce many men to leave the world for a life of prayer and devotion. Some of them were drop-outs from a society whose values they rejected, others were clergy who were persuaded by religious reformers to live a stricter life for the good of their souls. All of them had in principle renounced the secular world and vowed to live a communal life based on personal poverty, sexual abstinence and obedience to authority in the person of their abbot or prior. However austere the lives of their inmates may sometimes have been, medieval monasteries needed benefactors to give them sites and endowments, and there was a tendency for the patronage of the great to focus on one particular Order which for a generation would enjoy their bounty before losing its appeal in face of some newer and stricter manifestation of religious zeal. Thus in England the

Overleaf: The Beer Cellar showing the wooden racks upon which the barrels stood. Vast quantities of home-brewed beer were drunk by the household. In 1737, for instance, 120 hogsheads of small beer and 53 of strong beer were consumed, besides 1883 bottles of Port and other wines. A hogshead contained $52\frac{1}{2}$ gallons.

Benedictines were the Order favoured by the first generation of Norman barons after the Conquest, but by the middle of the twelfth century they had given way in aristocratic esteem to the Cistercians. The Austin canons were especially favoured by King Henry I (1100–1135) and his courtiers, and it was to a baron closely associated with Henry that Calke Priory owed its foundation. He was Richard, 3rd Earl of Chester, a young man who in 1101 had inherited vast estates from his father Earl Hugh d'Avranches. The heart of his lands was in Cheshire, but many manors on the borders of Derbyshire and Leicestershire also belonged to him, including Calke, Repton, Ticknall, Smisby and Newton Solney. At the time of his father's death he was only seven years old. He would have come of age in 1115, and some time between then and 1120, when he was one of a shipload of courtiers who were drowned while crossing the English Channel, he decided to found an Augustinian priory at Calke dedicated to St. Giles. No foundation charter has been preserved, but later Earls of Chester confirmed their predecessor's benefactions to the canons of Calke, and King Henry I and his grandson King Henry II both gave the priory royal protection. A letter of Henry II to this effect is one of the earliest documents to be preserved among the Harpur-Crewe archives.

It was important for religious houses to have the protection of kings and earls because in the twelfth century church property was not always respected by laymen and sometimes bitter disputes arose between one monastery and another. Thus at Calke the newly-founded priory soon found itself at odds with the powerful Benedictine abbey of St. Werburgh at Chester which, among other lands in Derbyshire, held the manor of Walton-on-Trent by the gift of Earl Hugh. Whereas the latter had been a great benefactor of St. Werburgh's, his son Earl Richard had the reputation of being no friend to the monks of Chester: indeed the foundation of Calke Priory was itself an indication that Richard's favours were being bestowed on a different sector of the monastic establishment. Exactly how the canons of Calke fell foul of the monks of Chester we do not know, but the latter may have had some dormant claim to lands or rights in the neighbourhood of Calke which the advent of the priory threatened to extinguish for ever. At all events serious friction arose between the two religious communities, in the course of which the monks went so far as to deprive the canons of their priory church. Eventually the canons won this ecclesiastical battle, and their victory was publicly proclaimed at a church council held in London some time in the 1130s. The three archbishops of the Anglo-Norman kingdom (Canterbury, York and Rouen) were all there, and in their presence the abbot of Chester formally abandoned his claims to Calke and promised that he would leave the canons in peace.

Although Calke Priory was successfully defended against the malice of the monks of Chester, it was not to retain its status as an independent religious community for many more years. After the death of the 5th Earl of Chester in 1153 some or all of the Derbyshire estate that he had inherited formed part of the dower of his widow Matilda. Early in the reign of King Henry II (1154–1189) the Countess Matilda made arrangements for the canons of Calke to move to a new site at Repton, five miles away beyond Ticknall. It is possible that the countess had a manor-house at Repton, but the fact that before the Danish invasions of the ninth century Repton had been the site of a famous Anglo-Saxon monastery no doubt influenced her decision. By this act the countess became in effect the foundress of Repton Priory, which she further endowed with lands in Huntingdonshire. By 1172 'the prior and canons of the Holy Trinity of Repton' were established in their new buildings and 'the prior and convent of St. Giles of Calke' had ceased to exist as an autonomous body.

What happened at Calke after the migration to Repton is uncertain. The Countess Matilda's charter implies that Calke was to continue to exist as a religious community, but subordinate to Repton: in other words it was to be what was called technically a 'cell', that is a satellite establishment with less than the full complement of canons. In the twelfth and early thirteenth centuries, when the religious orders were still attracting numerous recruits, a few canons may still have been in permanent residence at Calke, but in the later Middle Ages vocations declined in numbers and it is likely that in the fourteenth and fifteenth centuries Calke Priory was more important as the centre of an agricultural estate than as a religious community.

In the reign of Henry I, however, we must envisage Calke Priory as the home of a dozen or more canons, distinguished from members of other religious orders by their black outer garment. The buildings they occupied would have conformed to a standard plan of which the principal components were a church, a chapter-house, a refectory and a dormitory, grouped round a cloister. We can be sure that all these buildings were envisaged when Calke Priory was founded, and it is likely that some if not all of them were completed before the move to Repton. Whether all of them survived until the dissolution of the parent monastery in 1538 is another matter. Some adaptation or demolition is likely to have taken place in response to changing circumstances, and by the 1530s Calke may well have looked more like a manor-house than a monastery. But whatever its form and appearance in the last days of English monasticism, there is every reason to suppose that Calke Priory occupied the site of the present mansion, and it is highly probable that some of its masonry survives embedded in the latter's fabric. In the nineteenth century medieval stone coffins were disinterred immediately to the north of the house, and more medieval remains may well come to light in the course of the extensive repairs now (1985) in hand.

Although the monastic occupation of Calke came to an end in 1538, one legacy of the priory survived into modern times. This was the status of the parish of Calke in the eyes of the church. Although not themselves exempted (as some of the greater monasteries were) from the authority of the diocesan bishop, the prior and convent of Repton were evidently allowed to assume complete responsibility for the maintenance of services in the parish church of Calke, since there is no record of any clergy having been instituted

Seal of the peculiar of Calke.

there by the Bishop of Lichfield. Calke in fact constituted what came to be known as a 'peculiar jurisdiction', the word 'peculiar' being here used in its original sense of something private. The status of the parish as a 'peculiar' persisted after the Reformation. The lords of the manor took the place of the prior and appointed the officiating clergyman without any reference to the bishop. They also exercised such rights as the probate of wills (then normally the right of the bishop), nominating a commissary or 'official' to act on their behalf. The appointment of one such 'Official or Commissary General of the exempt or peculiar jurisdiction of Calke' is recorded in 1636, and an ivory seal exists with a Latin inscription declaring it to be the seal of 'the official of the peculiar jurisdiction of Calke'. At Dale Abbey near Ilkeston the Stanhope family exercised similar rights, and there a monument in the church commemorates the fourth Earl Stanhope, who died in 1855, as 'Lord of this manor, and Lay Bishop of this Church'. Although 'Lay Bishop' was a title to which the Harpurs did not presume to lay claim, the Bishop of Lichfield had no jurisdiction in the parish of Calke until peculiars were abolished by Acts of Parliament in 1836 and 1850. Since then Calke Church has been effectively a private chapel within the parish of Ticknall.

After the Dissolution

Between 1536 and 1540 all the monasteries in England were dissolved by King Henry VIII and his minister Thomas Cromwell and their lands were confiscated by the Crown. Repton Priory was due for dissolution in 1536, but managed to buy a temporary respite and did not fall until 1538. Meanwhile the canons were for the moment still in possession of their legal powers. Like the Greater London Council in similar circumstances, they took steps they would not normally have contemplated. One of these was to grant long leases of their property at a nominal rent in return for cash down. And so, on 29 August 1537, they leased their 'cell or manor of Calke' to one John Priest or Prest for 99 years. The rent for the first 59 years was pre-paid, that for the remaining 40 being at the rate of £6 13s. 4d. p.a. John Prest was a member of the London Grocers' Company who had already advanced money to the prior and convent to help them pay for their exemption from dissolution in 1536. He evidently wanted to retire to the country, and after securing the lease of Calke he lived there until his death in 1546. The will of 'John Priest of Calke in the Countie of Darbie, esquire', indicates that he was a man of some substance, who could leave money for various charitable purposes, and be buried with the due formality of a sermon 'by some well learned man', as well as a *cortège* of poor men wearing black gowns and carrying flaming torches. He left the residue of his lease to his daughter Frances, but stipulated that his widow Alice was to be allowed to live at Calke for the rest of her life. Having remarried, she and her second husband Richard Blackwell remained at Calke until her death in 1549, whereupon their place was taken by Frances and her husband William Bradbourne.

Meanwhile Repton Priory had finally been dissolved in 1538, and its lands were at the disposal of the Crown. Repton itself was acquired by Cromwell's steward, Thomas Thacker of Heage,

The Boudoir (so called only since 1886) is devoted chiefly to the display of china and the local Ticknall pottery. It also contains pictures by or after Old Masters.

near Belper. Thacker also put in a bid for Calke, but was disappointed: instead it was one of a number of estates that were granted to John Dudley, then Earl of Warwick and soon to be Duke of Northumberland, following his successful campaign against the Scots in 1547. What Dudley acquired was, of course, only the freehold of the manor, subject to the 99 year lease to the Prest family, from whom no rent was due until 1596. He immediately sold the property to John Beaumont of Grace-Dieu in Leicestershire and his second son Henry. In 1573 the Beaumont family parted with the freehold for £450, and within the next two years both freehold and leasehold interests in Calke were acquired by Richard Wendsley or Wennesley.

Richard Wendsley was a member of an old Derbyshire family which took its name from Wensley in Darley Dale. He was a pushing man who had twice been M.P. for Derbyshire and he was actively engaged in the marketing of lead from the mines in the Peak. Having bought Calke he 'did build divers edifices thereupon and did inhabit and dwell upon the same'. He also used the property as security for several major deals in lead. One of those to whom Calke was mortgaged in this way was Robert Bainbridge, and it was to Bainbridge that Wendsley eventually sold the estate in 1585. Bainbridge, a lawyer by training, was a man of substance in Derby who represented that town in Parliament in 1571, 1572 and 1586. He was one of the extreme Protestant Members who espoused the Presbyterian cause and refused to accept the Elizabethan church settlement. Their radical religious policies and their plain speaking in the House of Commons infuriated Queen Elizabeth, and in 1586 Bainbridge was sent to the Tower of London by her order. There his name, cut on the wall of the Beauchamp Tower in which he was confined, still testifies to his clash with authority four hundred years ago.

Bainbridge took up residence at Calke. It is possible that the place appealed to him because the fact that the bishop had no jurisdiction in the parish would enable him to worship in the Puritan manner without any interference. There is a hint of this in his will, where he directs that he is to be buried in a vault that he has made in Calke Church, and that his funeral is to take place 'without any worldly pomp or glory with the company of such godly Christians as use to come to our assemblys upon the Lord's Day'. After his death, which took place in about 1615, Calke went to his second son Robert, who in February 1622 sold it to Henry Harpur for £5350.

2 THE RISE OF A GENTRY FAMILY

The Founders of the Family

IN THE Harpur Chapel in Swarkeston Church there are two monuments of Derbyshire alabaster. They commemorate the founders of the family of which Henry Harpur was a member. The Harpurs had been minor gentry in Warwickshire and Staffordshire since the fourteenth century, but it was Henry's grandfather Richard who in the reign of Queen Elizabeth established his branch of the family as major landowners in south Derbyshire. Richard Harpur's immediate ancestors were the lords of Rushall, a village near Walsall in Staffordshire. His father Henry was a younger son of Sir John Harpur, who died in 1464, having rebuilt Rushall Church at his own expense. Richard studied law at Barnard's Inn in London and then moved on to the Inner Temple, where he was chosen to be the reader, an official lecturer in Law, in 1554. At the same time he would be practising as a pleader (the Tudor equivalent of a barrister). His success in this capacity led in 1558 to his promotion to the rank of serjeant. The serjeants-at-law were chosen by the Crown from the most able and promising pleaders and it was from their select ranks that the judges of the Court of Common Pleas were appointed. Richard Harpur's turn came in 1567, when he became one of the four judges of what was then the principal court for actions between private parties, especially for cases which involved real property. In addition he was in 1571 appointed Chief Justice of the County Palatine of Lancaster. In a litigious age he was at the top of his profession and his rewards were correspondingly great. As a serjeant he could command substantial fees for giving great men the benefit of his opinion. As a judge he could expect to earn an income whose modern equivalent would have to be estimated in tens of thousands of pounds. Not only did Mr. Serjeant Harpur have money to invest. His profession gave him unrivalled opportunities to observe the traffic in land and manorial rights that brought some men to wealth and others to ruin. It was experience that men like himself could turn to their own advantage when they considered how best to lay out their own money.

Just how Richard Harpur built up his estate remains to be worked out, but we have it on the authority of his wife that he 'did

The Breakfast Room, used latterly for afternoon tea. On the left are the views of Naples by Ricciardelli acquired by Sir Henry Crewe, and on the wall opposite are (above) 'The Exeter Mail Coach changing Horses', by William Davis (painted in 1821) and 'Kingsey Village near Thame', by J. Linnell (painted in 1826). The circular rosewood table came from Willington Grange, the home of Col. and Mrs. Mosley before the latter inherited Calke in 1924.

get his goods and lands with great travail and pain'. By the end of his life he owned property as far afield as Lancashire and Cheshire. He even owned one manor in the East Riding of Yorkshire. But the heart of his estate was in Derbyshire and Staffordshire. The Staffordshire estate (centred on Alstonfield, north of Ashbourne) he acquired by purchase, but most of the Derbyshire estate he acquired by marriage to the heiress of the Finderns, a family who had lived for centuries at the village five miles south-west of Derby from which they took their name.

When Richard Harpur married Jane Findern, probably in the late 1540s, we do not know whether she had any expectation of inheriting the family estate. Her father George had died in 1540, leaving her brother Thomas as his successor. At all events Thomas's death without children in 1558 left Jane as the heiress and Richard at once joined the ranks of the Derbyshire gentry as her husband. He was now the owner of lands in Findern, Swarkeston, Repton, Ticknall, Twyford, Stanton-by-Bridge and elsewhere in south Derbyshire. He chose to build a new house for himself at Swarkeston rather than live in the old manor-house at Findern, and during the remaining years of his life steadily amassed property in the neighbourhood. When he died in January 1577 he was buried in Swarkeston Church, in a chapel that he had built in his lifetime. The monument to himself and his wife is a late and clumsy product of a once well-known firm of carvers at Burton-on-Trent called Roiley. As a work of art it cannot be commended, but the featureless dummy that represents the founder of the Harpur family fortunes is correctly clothed in the robes of an Elizabethan judge, and his head is encased in the close-fitting linen cap or coif that was the distinctive headgear of a serjeant-at-law. Round his neck is the collar or chain that he would have worn as Chief Justice of Lancaster. He clasps a ribbon inscribed with the lugubrious motto of the Finderns: *Cogita mori* ('Think of death'), and on his right hand is a ring inscribed RH. In his will he left money for similar rings to be made and worn in his memory by the Lord Chief Justice of England and various family and professional friends.

As a good Protestant Richard Harpur provided for sermons to be preached after his death in the churches of Swarkeston, Chellaston and Barrow instead of the masses that would have been normal before the Reformation. His will also reflects the new concern for education that was felt by many of the Tudor gentry. Here personal and family connections came into play. When as a young lawyer Richard Harpur had been admitted to membership of the Inner Temple it was 'at the instance' of Sir John Port (d.1541), one of the judges of the King's Bench. Port was lord of the manor of Etwall only a few miles from Swarkeston. His daughter Elizabeth married George Findern and was Jane Harpur's mother. His son Sir John Port (d.1557) was accordingly the latter's uncle, and the younger Sir John was a 'dear friend' to Jane and her husband.

When Sir John Port made his will in 1556 he provided for the foundation of a grammar school at Repton and made Richard Harpur one of his executors. Richard Harpur was therefore personally involved in the establishment of Repton School, and in his

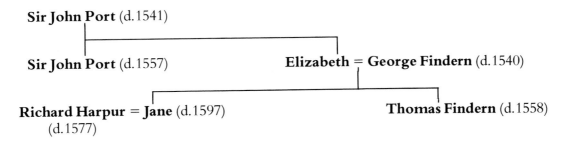

Sir John Port (d.1541)

Sir John Port (d.1557)   **Elizabeth** = **George Findern** (d.1540)

Richard Harpur = **Jane** (d.1597)   **Thomas Findern** (d.1558)
(d.1577)

Richard Harpur, the founder of the Harpur family fortunes, lies in effigy on his tomb in Swarkeston Church beside his wife Jane, the heiress of the Finderns.

will he left £30 for the maintenance of a scholar there. His descendants, as executors of the founder's will and the principal local landowners, became so closely involved with the management of the school that the head of the family has ever since been one of the four hereditary governors, the other three being descendants of Sir John Port's three daughters. Both the elder and the younger Port were benefactors to Brasenose College, Oxford, and in 1572 Richard Harpur followed their example by endowing a Greek Lectureship at the college. Several Harpurs were subsequently to be educated there, including Sir Henry (d.1639), the first baronet.

Richard and Jane Harpur left two sons, John and Richard. In the testament attached to her will Jane enjoined them to maintain that family solidarity which 'will be comfort to your friends and grief to your enemies', and so, as far as we know, they did. John, as

No motor-vehicle was allowed past the lodge gates until after the death of Sir Vauncey Harpur Crewe in 1924, and a marvellous collection of carriages survives to illustrate horse-drawn transport in the nineteenth and early twentieth centuries.

the elder, inherited Swarkeston and the bulk of his father's estates, while Richard was set up as lord of the manor of Littleover near Derby. There his descendants continued to live until that branch of the family became extinct in the middle of the eighteenth century.

John followed in his father's footsteps by entering the Inner Temple in 1564, but such legal education as he received was doubtless intended to equip him for his life as a country gentleman rather than as a professional lawyer. By 1573 he was a Justice of the Peace, and he soon became deeply involved in local government. This was a time when the Justices of the Peace formed the backbone of county administration, fulfilling many functions that in a later age were to be taken over by County Councils. In Derbyshire the active Justices numbered about twenty, and in due course Richard Harpur of Littleover and Robert Bainbridge of Calke were both brought onto the 'Quorum'. Formally Justices of the Peace were appointed by the Lord Chancellor, but he would often act on the recommendation of local magnates. In Derbyshire at this time the leading magnates were the Earls of Shrewsbury, who from Sheffield Castle exercised a close control over the affairs of the county. Judge Harpur had been consulted by the 6th Earl on legal and other matters. John Harpur continued to support him, both in his private affairs (especially his quarrel with his formidable wife, Bess of Hardwick), and in public life, and it was doubtless to Shrewsbury that Harpur owed his place on the Justices' bench. In the critical year of the Spanish Armada (1588) Shrewsbury regarded John Harpur as one of those 'in whom I put especial trust in county affairs', and when Gilbert Talbot succeeded as 7th Earl in 1590 Harpur became his right-hand man. As the Earl's agent he was employed in every aspect of administration, collecting loans and subsidies, mustering militiamen, raising troops for service in Ireland, and pursuing Papists.

Since the Catholic plot against the Queen's life and the Spanish attempt to invade her kingdom, English Papists were subject to penal laws and local Justices were expected to keep them under surveillance. John Harpur had his share of this distasteful work, which set up a barrier of hostility between Protestant gentlemen like himself and their Catholic neighbours. In this atmosphere of suspicion and delation it was easy to put a foot wrong, and in 1595 John Harpur got into very serious trouble indeed. It began when Robert Bainbridge, the ultra-Protestant owner of Calke, wrote a secret report to the Privy Council denouncing several of the Earl of Shrewsbury's servants and counsellors as 'notorious Papists and dangerous recusants' (the official term for those who refused to attend the services of the Established Church). John Harpur was not among those named by Bainbridge, but he was given the deeply embarrassing task of routing out a 'notable recusant' called Williamson who (according to Bainbridge) was 'maintained in a house of my Lord's [of Shrewsbury] at Sawley in the very heart of the shire'. Faced with a direct conflict between his duty to the state and his loyalty to his patron Harpur wavered: he privately warned Williamson of his danger, and gave him the opportunity to rid himself of some incriminating documents before

The Banqueting House at Swarkeston. This is a relic of the great house which was the principal seat of the Harpur family in the sixteenth and seventeenth centuries. It may be identical with a 'Bowl-alley house' built in 1630–2, and if so the walled forecourt would have been the bowling green.

the search took place. The result was that he was summoned to London to account for his actions, examined by the Attorney-General, and sent to the Fleet Prison, whence he addressed a series of abject letters to Sir Robert Cecil, the Secretary of State, protesting his loyalty to the Queen, his adherence to the Protestant faith and his penitence for his 'late error and great oversight'. 'The restraint of my liberty', he wrote, 'doth most heavily afflict me', and to a man who hitherto had 'lived free from all suspicion', the questioning of

his loyalty was 'a mortal wound to a clear conscience and innocent subject'. It was more than nine weeks before he was released and more than seven years before he was again to hold office as a Justice of the Peace.

In Derbyshire, however, John Harpur's credit was evidently not seriously damaged, for in 1597 (no doubt with Shrewsbury's backing) he was elected M.P. for the county in company with Thomas Gresley of Drakelow, whose daughter Catherine was married to his eldest son Richard. In the last year of Elizabeth's reign he was restored to the Bench, and in April 1603 he was knighted by James I. From 1605 he was Deputy to the Earl of Shrewsbury as Lord Lieutenant of Derbyshire and in 1604 he served as Sheriff of the County. Completely reinstated, he became once more a pillar of the Derbyshire establishment, arbitrating in a dispute between local landowners, taking preventative action against levellers and enclosure riots, helping Sir John Byron to put his affairs in order after the death of his father, attempting, in company with Sir John Bentley, to placate the 'giddy-headed' people of Glossopdale, who were disputing the terms of their leases under the Earl of Shrewsbury.

When he died in 1622 Sir John Harpur was one of the best-known and most respected figures in the county. The poet Thomas Bancroft wrote an epigram in his memory and when the dramatist William Sampson published a series of 'Epitomes of Honorable, Noble, Learned and Hospitable Personages' in 1636 under the title *Virtus Post Funera Vivit*, one of them was 'On the never-dying memory of ould Sir John Harper of Swarkeston'. In the Harpur Chapel he and his first wife lie beneath effigies of local alabaster commissioned by himself before his death and made by an unknown sculptor of some ability.

In Sir John Harpur's day Swarkeston was both a convenient and a pleasant place to live, not far from Derby and close by the bridge over the Trent which carried the main road south to Ashby-de-la-Zouch and Coventry. Here, where both air and water were as yet unpolluted by industry, salmon were to be caught in the river and hawks could be flown at herons feeding in its shallows. Neighbouring gentry would call on their way to or from Derby and occasionally the Earl of Shrewsbury himself might, in the course of a 'progress', accept Sir John's invitation to 'visit the sweet air of the country and be pleased to take in my house in your way'. Then the musicians would play, as they did for the Earl of Huntingdon in 1610, and the best plate would be got out in the great man's honour. Of the house itself we know little more than can be gleaned from an inventory of its contents drawn up by Sir John himself in 1620. Most of it has been demolished, but the adjoining Banqueting House survives, a delightful twin-towered building standing at one end of a walled enclosure that was probably a bowling green (see p. 29).

Sir John Harpur married twice. By his first wife Isabella, daughter of Sir George Pierrepont of Holme Pierrepont in Nottinghamshire, he had seven sons and five daughters. They are all drawn up in effigy on the side of his monument, but only one of the sons and four of the daughters survived their father. His eldest son Richard, knighted in 1617, died two years later, leaving a son John and three unmarried daughters. His second son John, who had become lord of the manor of Breadsall by marriage to the heiress of the Dethick family, died early in 1622, leaving a son aged ten. Two months later Sir John's grandson John, who had recently married the daughter and heiress of Sir Henry Beaumont of Grace-Dieu in Leicestershire, followed his father to the grave, barely leaving the old man time to draw up a new will before his own death on 8 October. As four of the remaining five sons had long since been dead, this left his third son Henry and his other grandson John (son of John of Breadsall) as his only male heirs. By the laws of primogeniture John took precedence over Henry, and in due course succeeded to the estate. In 1630, at the age of 18, he was knighted, and soon afterwards he was married to Catherine, daughter and heiress of the Hon. Henry Howard, a son of Thomas, Earl of Suffolk, by Elizabeth, sole daughter and heiress of Thomas Bassett of Blore in Staffordshire. This was a strategic marriage designed to bring the Blore estate near Ashbourne into the Harpur inheritance, but it failed in its purpose: John's only son Henry, born in 1639, was to die before his father.

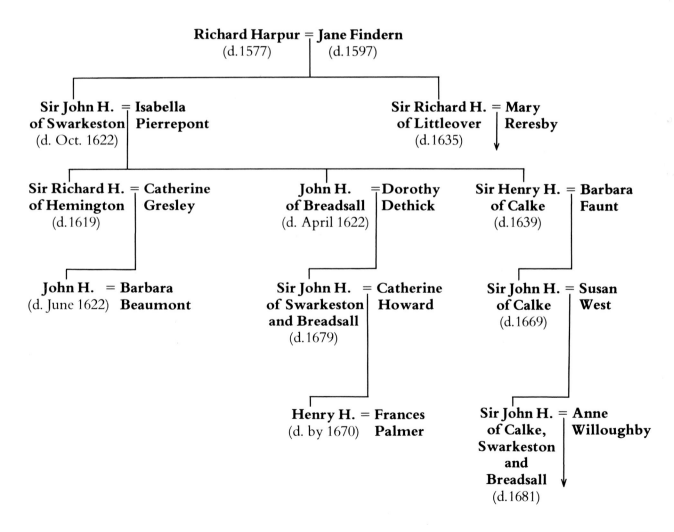

Sir John Harpur had scarcely come of age before the tensions that were to lead to the Civil War began to build up around him. Derbyshire was a county where royal exactions were strongly resisted. As early as 1626 a 'benevolence'* had been almost unanimously refused by its people and in the early 1630s resistance to Ship Money was widespread. In 1636 Sir John was appointed Sheriff, and in that capacity had the responsibility for enforcing the latest royal demands. The Ship Money assessment for the county was £3500, and of this he succeeded in collecting all but £100. To show his zeal he sent up the whole sum of £3500 to the Council, only asking to be given credit for the balance if he met with 'absolute refusal' to pay it. No doubt it was natural that one whose family had been for so long the agents of royal authority in Derbyshire should himself be a Royalist, and in 1642 he and his cousin, Sir John Harpur of Calke, both made their loyalties clear by signing a protest to Sir John Gell, who was organising the Parliamentary party in the county. Early in the following year, learning that the Royalists were fortifying Swarkeston, Gell sent a strong force to take this important crossing of the Trent. The Royalists immediately abandoned the house, but there was a fight before the bridge was captured on 5 January 1643.

The 'Battle of Swarson Bridge' meant the end of active resistance by Sir John Harpur and his men. Its owner was now classed as a 'delinquent' whose property was liable to sequestration and sale. However it was open to him to 'compound' for his estate by paying a fine whose severity was proportionate to the degree of 'delinquency' he was deemed to have shown. After the Restoration Sir John Harpur was described as 'well affected to the King and Church but backward in acting for either', and the assessment of one tenth of the value of his property (calculated on the basis of two years' income) showed that in the 1640s he was not regarded as a determined opponent of the Parliamentary regime. The fine payable was (after various adjustments) declared to be £4583. This Sir John had paid by May 1649. He claimed that he was already in debt to the extent of £13,000 and that some land would have to be sold to raise the money for the fine. Meanwhile his estate had suffered from depredation: he estimated the damage done to his 'houses, personal estate and woods' at £8000.

Despite these losses Sir John Harpur was still a rich man: indeed the fine he paid in 1649 indicates that he was one of the wealthiest of the Derbyshire gentry. In his dealings with the Committee for Compounding, Sir John Harpur would no doubt have understated his income, but in any case it was well above the average for his class, and after the Restoration he could once more enjoy it without fear either of royal exaction or of parliamentary confiscation. In 1661 he was made a Deputy Lieutenant, but he did not serve again as Sheriff. He died on 20 February 1679, aged about 66, appointing as sole executrix his second wife Frances, daughter of Lord Willoughby of Parham. To her care he entrusted 'the solemnisation of my Funeral in such decent manner as becomes the funeral of a person of my degree and quality'. By a settlement made in 1670 after the death of his only son Henry, his heir was his cousin Sir John Harpur of Calke.

* A 'benevolence' was nominally a free gift to the Exchequer but in fact an exaction. Ship Money was a tax, for naval purposes, of doubtful legality.

The First Three Baronets

When Sir John Harpur of Calke succeeded to the Swarkeston estate in 1679 he was a young man in his thirties and Calke had been the property of his branch of the family for over 50 years. His grandfather Henry Harpur had bought the estate from Robert Bainbridge in 1622. The transaction – or the money with which to effect it – was clearly part of the family settlement made by Sir John Harpur of Swarkeston before his death in October 1622 and alluded to in his will. 'I have given and conveyed unto my son Henry Harpur', he wrote, 'divers lands and tenements of good value in full discharge and satisfaction of such child's part or portion as he may . . . claim'. As the purchase of Calke cost £5350, Henry could not complain of the way in which he had been treated. Born in about 1579, he had been educated at Brasenose College, Oxford, for two years before being entered at the Inner Temple in 1598. He married a young widow: Barbara, daughter of Anthony Faunt of Foston in Leicestershire, whose first husband, Sir Henry Beaumont of Grace-Dieu in

This magnificent chimney-piece dates probably from the late sixteenth century and is believed by family tradition to have been brought from the old Harpur mansion at Swarkeston. If so the coat of arms must be a later insertion as it incorporates the insignia (a red hand) of the baronetcy granted to Sir Henry Harpur of Calke in 1626. The arms displayed are intended to emphasise the antiquity of the family and include the Harpurs' own lion rampant and the Finderns' chevron and crosses. On top is the family crest, described in the quaint heraldic language as 'a Boar passant or, collared and bristled gules'.

the same county, had died in 1605. Her dower would have made the match financially attractive and her infant Beaumont daughter was later married to one of Henry's nephews.

In 1625 Henry Harpur held office as Sheriff of Derbyshire, and in 1626 he secured for himself and his descendants the hereditary dignity of a baronet. This new title had been created by James I in 1611 as a way of raising money. Only gentlemen who had land worth at least £1000 a year were to be eligible, and the number of baronets was to be strictly limited to 200. The titles cost £1095 each and by the end of James I's reign all 200 had been sold. But Charles I's financial difficulties induced him to reopen the list, and Henry Harpur was one of those who bid for the newly-available title. At the time there were only four other baronets in Derbyshire, but Sir Thomas Burdett of adjoining Foremark was one, and so was his near neighbour Sir Henry Shirley of Staunton Harold in Leicestershire. It may well have been their example that he sought to emulate. Although his credentials as a gentleman were unimpeachable, it is doubtful whether his estate was worth as much as £1000 a year. But ready money was the essential requirement. Altogether the honour cost him £1395 – £1095 payable to the Exchequer, and £300 to Dr. John Moore, a man in the service of the Duke of Buckingham who acted as an intermediary between those seeking honours and his master, who at this time was the chief dispenser of royal patronage.

Apart from this demonstration of social ambition all we know of the first Harpur owner of Calke is that in 1624 the musical composer Francis Pilkington chose to dedicate to him his *Second Set of Madrigals and Pastorals*, presumably an indication that in the reign of James I music was a favourite diversion at Calke.

When Sir Henry Harpur died in 1639 he left three sons and six daughters. In his will he expressed concern that his widow's dower, plus the portions he had provided for his younger children, would leave his eldest son John 'very little or nothing to maintain himself withall'. John may certainly have had a lean time until his mother's death ten years later brought her dower back into the estate. Meanwhile other troubles had supervened. In 1640 undisciplined Royalist soldiers from Ashby, 'councelled and animated' by the inhabitants of Ticknall and Calke, ran amok in the neighbourhood. Rightly or wrongly Sir John Harpur was suspected of complicity in these disorders. In the following year he had the difficult task of serving as Sheriff in a county by now largely hostile to royal authority. Although his sympathies were unquestionably Royalist he played no significant part in the Civil War, and, unlike his cousin at Swarkeston, escaped denunciation as a 'delinquent'. Nevertheless his record was suspect, and when in 1649 'delinquents' who failed to compound were warned that they risked the forfeiture of their estates, he submitted to the Committee for Compounding, and was fined on the basis of one year's income, assessed at £578 18s. 2d. He lived to see the Restoration and died in 1669 aged 53. He directed that his body should be buried in the church at Calke, 'decently and with a moderate expense'. No monument had been erected to his father's memory, nor was one made for him, but for many years a

Portrait of Sir John Harpur 2nd Baronet who died in 1669, aged 53, painted as a memorial to hang in the church.

framed portrait of him hung in Calke Church. It shows him with his hand on a skull and was evidently painted as a memorial. In the nineteenth century it was removed to the house in order to preserve it from damage by damp and now to be seen hanging in the Saloon (see previous page).

Sir John Harpur had five sons and five daughters. The title and the main body of the estate descended to his eldest son John. John had been educated at Queen's College, Oxford, where he had as his tutor Joseph Williamson, soon to be Secretary of State to Charles II. In 1674 he married Anne, third daughter of Lord Willoughby of Parham, whose sister Frances had married, as his second wife, Sir John Harpur of Swarkeston. As the latter marriage had been childless, and as Sir John's only son by his first marriage predeceased him, his heir was his cousin of Calke. By 1679, therefore, the three Harpur estates centred on Swarkeston, Breadsall and Calke devolved on one person: the somewhat impecunious baronet of Calke had become one of the richest men in Derbyshire, with lands in four counties and a rent-roll of over £3000 a year. He was not to enjoy his new wealth for long. *Cogita Mori* was still the family motto, and on 12 August 1681 Sir John Harpur died at the age of 36. He left two infant children, John, aged about fifteen months, and a daughter Anne. Provided he survived the perils of childhood, John would inherit all the Harpur properties. But it would be nearly twenty years before he came of age and meanwhile the estate was managed by guardians appointed under his father's will. Their accounts (kept by John Harpur of Twyford, son of the first baronet's younger son William) show that every year there was a substantial surplus. By 1701, when the heir would reach the age of 21, he would have some £40,000 in hand, besides a regular annual income of between £2000 and £3000 – equivalent to well over £100,000 a year in modern currency. He had reason to be satisfied with his guardians' management, and one of his first acts on coming of age was to give them a present of £1500 each for their trouble. John Harpur of Twyford received a similar sum in recognition of his 'extraordinary pains and trouble'.

On 23 March 1701 the bells of all the churches between Derby and Ashby-de-la-Zouch were ringing to celebrate the coming-of-age of the young baronet of Calke. From Breadsall in the north to Smisby in the south, from Burton-on-Trent in the west to Hemington in the east, the peals proclaimed the extent of Harpur wealth and Harpur influence. Altogether there were 21 bands of ringers who claimed their reward for ringing-in the new owner of Calke. At Derby and Lichfield there were drummers too. At Calke itself the occasion, we are told, was 'kept with great solemnity'.

For Sir John it was the end of his tutelage and the start of a new and privileged life as a member of the English aristocracy. In England the aristocracy was never a closed caste: it was constantly being recruited from below, from the ranks of the gentry, just as the ranks of the gentry were themselves being recruited from the professions, and to a lesser extent from trade. The sixteenth century had been a great forcing-ground of gentry and aristocracy alike.

Into the Aristocracy

Many ancient families had been destroyed by Tudor tyranny, and many new families were built on the ruins of their estates and those of the monasteries. Lawyers in particular throve, and the Harpurs were only one of many landed families whose founder was a judge. Throughout the seventeenth century they were established members of the Derbyshire gentry. They held the offices of Justice of the Peace, Sheriff and Deputy Lieutenant which marked their status as substantial landowners in their county, and when they married they married the sons and daughters of other gentry: Bassetts, Beaumonts, Gilberts, Lowes, Palmers, Pierreponts and Wilmots. By purchasing a baronetcy Henry Harpur of Calke had made a bid for a slightly higher status than his income could support. Now, by the accidents of death, the entire Harpur inheritance had come into the hands of his great-grandson, and an altogether new life-style was within the latter's grasp: a life-style that, without of course severing his Derbyshire roots, would bring him into contact with the wider world of the English aristocracy. Like all life-styles it had no precise specification. But a prestigious country mansion was a basic requirement. There the great man could display his wealth, exert his influence and preside over his family and dependants. A permanent house in London was another: for London was the home of the Court, and the Court was still the focus of social and political life. Only by spending several months in London each year could one attend those royal levees which were open to men of rank and fortune and participate in the social life of the capital. Then, as now, a new and impressive vehicle was a universal status-symbol: a coach and four was as obvious a manifestation of wealth as a Rolls-Royce is today. Liveried servants were, of course, essential, and so was a display of silver on buffet or dining-table. A fine library, a gallery of pictures, a racing stable, a herd of deer, were optional extras, to be adopted according to taste. But in the choice of a wife the greatest care was requisite: here both rank and wealth were important, rank to support or even to enhance one's own, and wealth to add to the family inheritance.

Within a few years of his coming of age Sir John had acquired many of these symbols of aristocratic affluence. He had rebuilt his house on a scale commensurate with his wealth and standing in the county. He had furnished it fashionably with walnut chairs and damask hangings. He had bought silver from Paul de Lamerie and plants from London and Wise. Above all he had married well. The lady whom he chose for his wife was Catherine, daughter of the second Lord Crewe of Steane in Northamptonshire. She was the youngest of her father's four daughters, and as his successor Nathaniel Crewe, the elderly Bishop of Durham, had no children, it was fairly certain that she and her sisters would be co-heiresses of the substantial Crewe estates in Northamptonshire. Meanwhile she brought with her a marriage-portion of £12,000. On both counts, therefore, she was an eligible match for a young baronet anxious to break into aristocratic society. She herself was less happy about the marriage: indeed, she told her friends that 'one had better to be buried alive than married to one that gives disgust'. However she had a generous allowance of £400 a year in 'pin-

This wine-cistern is the outstanding piece of silver at Calke. Elaborately decorated in a baroque style, it was the work of Paul de Lamerie, a celebrated silversmith of French Huguenot origin, and was made in 1719. Although de Lamerie was certainly employed by Sir John and Catherine Lady Harpur (for whom he made an almsdish for the church), this wine-cistern may have been acquired by a later member of the family, as the arms of Harpur above the spigot were not engraved until much later in the eighteenth century.

money' and she made it a condition of her consent that she should be allowed to spend some months in town every year. The wedding must have been a suitably splendid event. Lady Harpur's dress cost £700, and round her neck there hung a diamond necklace purchased for the occasion for £960.

However little Catherine Harpur cared for her husband, she duly bore him six children between 1704 and 1713. For his part, he faithfully fulfilled his promise as to residence in London. In 1706 he spent £930 on purchasing a house at 26, St. James's Place,

The charming portraits of the children of Sir John and Catherine Lady Harpur were both painted in 1718. On the left, Henry (the eldest) and John, by Charles D'Agar; on the right Edward and Catherine by John Verelst.

overlooking the Green Park, and close to one occupied since 1698 by his friends and neighbours the Cokes of Melbourne. For some years his steward carefully recorded the dates when the family set out on the four-day journey to London and when they returned to Calke. In 1711–12 they were away for nearly six months – from 22 October to 12 April. In 1713 they did not set out until early in the New Year, returning on 16 May. In 1714 they were away from 12 January to 20 May, in 1715 from 9 March to 27 May, and in 1716 from 21 February to 7 June.

In public life Sir John Harpur made no mark. In 1701 he was doubtless too busy with his own affairs to think of standing for Parliament, and it was his cousin, John Harpur of Twyford, who was elected M.P. for Derby in that year and again in 1702. The electoral situation in Derbyshire at this time was as follows: two Members were returned for the county, and two for the borough of Derby. Politically speaking the dominant families were the Whig Cavendishes in the north and the Tory Curzons in the south. This balance of power was rarely upset, as neither family could afford the expense of contesting every election. So there was a member of the Curzon family in every parliament from 1701 to 1761, and from 1734 onwards the Cavendishes held one seat continuously until 1830. The Harpurs were Tories and in 1701–2 Derby was represented by one Tory (John Harpur) and one Whig (Lord James Cavendish, succeeded by Thomas Stanhope). At the next election in 1705 John Harpur was defeated, but in 1710 he shared in the great Tory victory of that year: he and Sir Richard Levinge 'carried [Derby] by a very great majority against my Lord James Cavendish and Mr. Pye'.

For his cousin's triumph Sir John could take no credit. Writing to her husband, Vice-Chamberlain Coke, from Melbourne, the latter's wife Elizabeth reported in September that 'Sir John they say cannot bear the name of election' and that, despite Lady Harpur's efforts, he had done little or nothing to rally his tenants in support of the Tory cause. After John Harpur's death in 1713 the family played no further part in county politics until 1734, when the passing of Walpole's Excise Bill made him so unpopular that the Tories thought they had a chance of winning all four seats. So Sir John's son Henry was put up as a second Tory candidate for the county, but came bottom of the poll. Richard Harpur of Littleover stood for one of the borough seats at Derby, but was equally unsuccessful. Sir John's distaste for politics can only have been strengthened by the outlay of £1245 11s. 4½d. on beer, bribery and bell-ringing which his son's candidature had cost him.

The shrievalty was, however, an office which Sir John could not well refuse, least of all in the year following the one in which he had succeeded to one of the largest estates in the county. In 1702–3 he accordingly served as High Sheriff of Derbyshire. By now the office was largely ceremonial, but it involved its holder in a good deal of trouble and expense. At the Assizes he appeared in state supported by his fellow gentry and accompanied by halberdiers, men in livery, and other functionaries, all of whom had to be regaled with venison pasties, beer and ale. The gaoler, the warders, even the prisoners, had to be fed at the Sheriff's expense throughout the Assizes, and when they were over the Under Sheriff, gaoler, bailiff and their respective wives expected a dinner on the 'execution day'. After the felons had been duly hanged the burial of their corpses and the tolling of the bell were 'at the Sheriff's charge'. Finally the poor of the town expected a distribution of alms, and the judge's servants 'will also crave a gratuity, though they dare not demand it'. The cost of all this to Sir John in 1702–3 was no less than £1529 18s. 11½d.

Not unnaturally gentlemen who were nominated for the shrievalty tended to excuse themselves, and those who had least influence in high places were left to bear the burden of the office. In 1690 a number of the Derbyshire gentry had made a compact not to seek to avoid serving their turn, and also to support the Sheriff in office by accompanying him in person and by each providing one man to form part of his liveried escort. As he was still a minor at the time, Sir John Harpur was naturally not a party to this agreement, but he may have benefited from it when he filled the office himself, and his cousin Richard Harpur of Littleover (who served as Sheriff in 1728) was a signatory to a similar compact in 1736. As a substantial landowner in Staffordshire Sir John was liable to be nominated as Sheriff for that county as well as for Derbyshire. His name was

The monument in Calke Church to Sir John Harpur (d.1741) and his wife Catherine Crewe, made by the sculptor Sir Henry Cheere in 1746. The iron rails were supplied by Robert Bakewell.

A collection of eighteenth and nineteenth-century wallets and writing-pads.

put forward in 1705 and again in 1711, but on both occasions he contrived to avoid being 'pricked'.

When William Woolley compiled his *History of Derbyshire* in about 1715 he wrote that the Harpurs were 'now accounted the best landed family of any commoners in this or any neighbouring county'. A valuation of Sir John Harpur's estate made in 1709 shows that he had some £4500 a year at his disposal, but by the 1730s this had increased by about £800. An income of over £5000 a year, though far below that of men like the Duke of Devonshire or the Duke of Rutland, put the Harpurs at the top of the scale for wealthy gentry. So Sir John Harpur, who had already made his sister's fortune up to £10,000 when she married in 1699, was able to give each of his three daughters a portion of £8000 each. His two younger sons were provided with incomes amounting to some £400 a year each. His wife was to have £1500 a year after his death, and the house in St. James's Place was hers for life. In the will that he drew up in 1734 he enjoined his eldest son Henry to ensure that his 'most tender and affectionate mother' received her money without any trouble or expense.

Sir John Harpur died suddenly at Calke on 24 June 1741, aged 61. His widow retired to live in Luffenham in Rutland, where she died in January 1745. In her will she enjoined her son to spend £150 on a 'plain monument' to his father in Calke Church. 'I will have no sort of monument myself' she declared, but in the end Sir Henry paid the sculptor Cheere £200 for a handsome marble monument surmounted by busts of both his parents. Lady Harpur's request and some other expressions in her will suggest that her initial 'disgust' at her marriage had given way to the marital respect and affection that is claimed in the funeral inscription.

Sir John left three sons and three daughters. The daughters all made good marriages to Midland landowners of standing: Jemima to Sir Thomas Palmer, Bart., of Carlton, Northants., Catherine to another baronet, Sir Henry Gough of Edgbaston, Warwickshire, Mary to Sir Lester Holte of Aston Hall in the same county. The two younger sons did less well. John disgraced himself in more ways than one, and when he died in 1780 his corpse 'was attended by no member of the Harpur family, and the only person who accompanied it was an old housekeeper who had promised to see the deceased safely buried'. Edward (1713–61) married and lived in Nottingham. He had been educated at Corpus Christi College in Cambridge, where his tutor complained of 'his keeping too much in his Rooms' and 'refusing all Company'. It was the first intimation of that congenital unsociability that was later to be so characteristic of his family.

While his younger brothers were living on their modest incomes, the new baronet was enjoying the possession of a great estate. He had been prepared for it by an education at Brasenose College, followed by the foreign travel that by now was *de rigueur* for those who could afford it. Most of his Grand Tour appears to have been spent in France, where his polite studies included the *manège*, or art of horsemanship. After his marriage in 1734 to Lady Caroline Manners, a daughter of the Duke of Rutland, he lived chiefly on Manners property at Bloxholme in Lincolnshire, until his father's death in 1741 brought him back to Calke. But Sir Henry had only seven years as head of the family before he too was laid in his grave at Calke Church: he was within a few weeks of his 40th

The front of the stables built in 1712–16.

birthday. He left two sons and two daughters, all under age. Both sons were sent to Westminster School (then much favoured by the elite). The younger (Charles) then went on to Christ Church, Oxford, before obtaining a Commission in the Army, while the elder (Henry, generally known as 'Harry') made the Grand Tour with his Swiss Protestant tutor, M. Louis de Crousaz.

Sir Harry's coming of age in 1760 was an event comparable to that of his grandfather in 1701. 'Last Saturday', reported the *London Chronicle* for 10–12 July, 'being the birthday of Sir Henry Harpur, Bart. who then being of age came into possession of a very large estate, the greatest rejoicings were made at Caulk-hall in Derbyshire ever known upon the like occasion: many thousands of Sir Henry's tenants and neighbours were present, and tents and other conveniences prepared for the reception of all without distinction: a fat ox, great plenty of venison, and provisions of every sort, with 90 hogsheads of strong beer, the utmost plenty of punch, and wines of various sorts, were provided for their entertainment: bands of music were provided for different sets of dancers, [and] the bells of all the neighbouring towns rang incessantly'.

Two years later Sir Harry married the Earl of Warwick's 'beautiful daughter', Lady Frances Greville. She brought him a portion of £5000. As a widow she was to receive £1200 a year, later increased to £1500 under her husband's will. Her mother-in-law Lady Caroline had the same, but Lady Frances enjoyed £500 a year in 'pin-money' during her husband's lifetime, whereas Lady Caroline had only £300.

Neither of the two Georgian baronets shared Sir John's distaste for politics. When, in July 1743, Sir Henry was made a Gentleman of the Privy Chamber to King George II, it was probably intended as a political overture from the Whig administration to a potential opponent. If so it was ineffectual, for early in the following year there was a by-election at Worcester and Sir Henry put himself forward as a Tory candidate and won the seat. Worcester was a politically independent borough which normally returned a local man, and what (apart from an expenditure by Sir Henry of £1226 on entertainment) induced the freemen to elect a Derbyshire baronet is not clear. At the general election in 1747 he transferred to Tamworth, where Lord Middleton, an old family friend, was High Steward and enjoyed the predominant political influence. Membership of Parliament necessitated a London residence, and as his mother had the house in St. James's Place for life, Sir Henry bought himself another in Upper Grosvenor Street (No. 35). His parliamentary career was terminated by his death in June 1748. His court appointment (which was purely honorific, involving no duties whatever) carried with it the privilege of exemption from local office, which doubtless explains why Sir Henry was the first owner of Calke since 1622 who did not serve as Sheriff of Derbyshire.

As for Sir Harry, he stood for Parliament at the first opportunity. In 1761 he was returned unopposed for the County of Derby and together with Lord George Cavendish represented it for the next seven years. He did not, however, play a very active part in

Sir Harry Harpur (d. 1789): a mezzotint by J. R. Smith.

Three eighteenth-century racing cups. The upper one (by Boulton and Fothergill of Birmingham) commemorates the success of Sir Harry Harpur's bay colt Cripple at Lichfield in 1776, and the other two (by Smith and Sharp of London), victories at Doncaster in 1774 and 1775.

political life: indeed he appears never to have spoken in the House of Commons and is recorded to have voted only once. When he offered himself for re-election in 1768 he was defeated by Godfrey Bagnall Clarke of Sutton near Chesterfield, who had the support of 'all the Tory gentlemen' in the county. In 1774 he served his turn as Sheriff with a good grace. The *Derby Mercury* reported:

> On Tuesday Sir Harry Harpur our High Sheriff gave an Invitation to the Grand Jury and a great number of Gentlemen, Tradesmen, etc., to dine with him at the George Inn, where the most elegant Entertainment was provided. In the evening he gave a free Ball to the Ladies at the New Assembly Rooms, at which the Company was both numerous and genteel and there was the greatest profusion of sweetmeats, wines, etc., that ever was known on such an occasion. The whole was conducted with the greatest Regularity and Decorum and the Company broke up about 2 o'clock highly pleased with the Munificence and polite behaviour of the High Sheriff and his Lady. And this morning a great number of poor people were bountifully relieved by Lady Frances Harpur.

In private life both Sir Henry and Sir Harry were enthusiastic owners and breeders of race-horses. Their horses were regularly seen at Newmarket and at most of the other principal race-meetings, and although neither of them ever won any of the major races, such as the St. Leger or The Oaks, they had their share of successes. Sir Henry won a gold cup at Chester in 1744 with his horse *Darling*. Sir Harry won at Doncaster in 1774 and again in 1775 with *Juniper*, at Richmond in 1775 with *Pilot*, at Lichfield in 1776 with *Cripple*, and again at Doncaster in 1777 with *Pilot*. Some of these horses subsequently earned substantial fees at stud. *Juniper*, for instance (a horse bought from the Duke of Cumberland in 1773), covered mares at Calke from 1777 to 1783 at 20 or 25 guineas, *Jason*

The State Bed

One of the most spectacular of Calke's hidden treasures is the State Bed, which has lain in pieces in a huge packing-case ever since it reached the house in the eighteenth century. According to family tradition it was a gift from Caroline, Queen of George II, to Lady Caroline Manners on the latter's marriage to the future Sir Henry Harpur in September 1734. How Lady Caroline earned this mark of royal favour is not clear, but Glover's assertion (in his *History of Derbyshire*, 1833) that she had been one of the Queen's bridesmaids is certainly wrong, as she had not been born at the time of the Queen's marriage in 1705. She had, however, been one of the bridesmaids when Princess Anne married the Prince of Orange in March 1734, and the bed may have been a royal present to her on the occasion of her own wedding six months later. Never having been exposed to the light, the hangings are in absolutely pristine condition. They are of Chinese silk, embroidered with conventionalised dragons, deer, etc., in colours which retain all their original brilliance.

Portrait of the 'isolated baronet' as a young man, drawn in pastels by Sir Thomas Lawrence.

(another purchase from the Duke) at 10 to 15 guineas. Several of Sir Harry's horses were the offspring of celebrated stallions such as *Snap* and *Goldfinder*. The latter horse belonged to Sir Charles Sedley of Nuthall Temple, Nottinghamshire, and in 1778, the last year of its owner's life, appears to have temporarily joined the Calke stud, where he covered twelve mares at £21 each.

Neither Sir Henry nor Sir Harry spent much on the fabric of the house at Calke or on embellishing its interior; but the latter began the landscaping of the park that was to be continued by his son, and it was he who introduced the Portland sheep that have been a feature of the place ever since. Many of the portraits of race-horses by Sartorius and Sawrey Gilpin that decorate the library were commissioned by Sir Harry, and it was at Calke, in company with Gilpin, that the water-colour painter John Smith (1749–1831) first met Sir Harry's brother-in-law the Earl of Warwick, who became so much Smith's patron that the latter was known for the rest of his life as 'John (Warwick) Smith'. Another youthful painter encouraged by the Harpurs was the future Sir Thomas Lawrence. He was the son of an innkeeper at Devizes, and Sir Harry and Lady Frances were among those en route for Bath who admired his precocious talent. Sir Harry was willing to pay for his artistic education in Italy, but Lawrence's father refused the offer. Pastel portraits of Sir Harry and his son, made by Lawrence at the age of about 15, hang in the Drawing Room.

As Members of Parliament the Georgian owners of Calke were of course much in London, and, not content with his town-house in Upper Grosvenor Street, Sir Harry provided himself with a suburban seat, first Tadworth Court in Surrey, which he bought in 1772 and sold four years later, and then Putney Park, which he leased from Lord Spencer from 1784 until his death in 1789.

These were all luxuries that the baronets of Calke could easily afford. Throughout the second half of the eighteenth century their estate steadily increased in value. In the 1750s it brought in an annual income of over £7000, and in the 1770s Sir Harry had at his disposal at least £10,000 a year. This put the Harpurs into an income bracket reserved for the four hundred wealthiest families in the country. With wives from Belvoir and Warwick Castles they were by now fully accepted as members of the English aristocracy. They lacked only a peerage title of their own to match their wealth and status. For this their dim political record was no recommendation, but Sir John's marriage to the co-heiress of a baron was a tenuous link with the peerage of which the family never lost sight. Meanwhile the death in 1721 of the last Lord Crewe (Nathaniel, Bishop of Durham) had brought the manor of Hinton (Northants.) into the Harpurs' hands. Until her death in 1745 it belonged to Sir John's widow, but in 1748 it was sold for £10,000, of which £7800 went to her two surviving daughters and their husbands, and £200 to her two younger sons.

3 THE WORLD OF THE HARPUR CREWES

The Isolated Baronet

SIR HARRY HARPUR was a bluff, open-handed gentleman for whom shooting, racing and coursing were the essence of life: as an old poacher who remembered him put it, he was 'a kind soul and a good sportsman'. Lady Frances, on the other hand, was a pious woman who became first a zealous Evangelical, then a frequenter of the Countess of Huntingdon's chapels, and at last a member of the Moravian sect. For her, life was a series of trials sent by God to prove her faith. She was, poor woman, to have ample opportunity to show her submissiveness to the Divine Will. The first was in 1789, when her husband died at the age of 50. For some time he had been suffering from gout and as the disease grew worse he became more and more averse to company. All attempts to persuade him to go to Buxton to try the effects of the waters were in vain, and although he bore his illness patiently enough, Lady Frances could not comfort herself that he did so from any 'Principle of Resignation'. When at last he died in February 1789, it was, alas, 'without a thought for Eternity'. Worse was to come. Sir Harry's only son and heir was another Henry, a young man of 25 who had been educated at Christ Church before embarking on a Grand Tour carefully planned for him by that M. de Crousaz who had been his father's tutor. After visiting the principal Italian cities he was to spend some time at Lausanne before returning by way of France. There he met M. de Crousaz who, writing to his mother, remarked not only on a 'fond d'instruction au delà de ce que j'en vois chez la plupart des jeunes Anglais qui sortent de leur pays', but also on an unhealthy 'goût pour la retraite'.*

As soon as he became owner of Calke, this shy young man withdrew from all the conventional contacts with society that were expected of a man in his position. For his mother, still for the moment in residence at Calke, it was even more distressing to find that her son 'has no religion, does not even go to church', and

---

* 'a fund of knowledge beyond what I notice among most of the young Englishmen who go abroad', ... 'taste for solitude'.

Miniature portrait of Sir Henry
Harpur, the 'isolated baronet'.

considered that all that mattered was 'being just in conduct ... and
inoffensive to others'. Lady Harpur was an indefatigable corres-
pondent, and it is through her pained eyes that we witness the next
development in Sir Henry's abdication of normal aristocratic standards. Writing to her friend Mrs. Dickinson of Taxal in May 1791,
she reported that 'my son has an unfortunate connection which
began last summer at Eastbourne. The Person is a Lady's maid, but
she has been from a child in good families, and more as a Com-
panion than servant, is young and pretty.... He is violently
attached to her. He has had her near 10 months ... She is at a house
near Caulke, but not in sight of it ... He sometimes dines at his great
house with a few friends, but nobody sees him...' 'My Brother',
she went on, 'thinks it a disgrace to his family and that he is lost to
the world ... and never would be persuaded to mix in society and
marry suitably ... He has no vices and many good qualities, but will
not be a man of the world'. In December an illegitimate daughter
was born, and in February 1792 Sir Henry committed the ultimate
indiscretion of marrying his mistress. Nanny Hawkins became
Lady Harpur. Needless to say she brought no money with her, but a
marriage settlement was drawn up whereby she was to have £200 a
year in 'pin money' and a jointure of £600 after her husband's death.

Though for Sir Henry's pious mother, her son's marriage came as a relief in so far as it regulated an immoral relationship, to the world in general it was a *mésalliance* that breached all the established conventions of Georgian society. Poor Lady Frances tried to make the best of the situation. After further acquaintance she decided that the new Lady Harpur was 'a very sensible pleasing young woman, her manners such as you would expect in superior rank, fond of domestic employment, has no wish for London or gayeties'. It was just as well that she did not hanker after 'gayeties', for Sir Henry still showed no disposition to take his place in society. On the contrary he 'would not suffer any Man, Friend or Servant to see his wife'. So far Lady Frances herself, though deeply distressed by his conduct, had remained on good terms with her son. She was now living in London, at 35 Park Street, but came down to Calke from time to time. As time went on, however, it was made clear to her that her visits were unwelcome, and in the end all contact with her daughter-in-law and grandchildren was forbidden. No doubt her son found her complaints of 'the want of Gospel Preaching and useful society' at Calke tiresome, but his refusal even to allow her to call on his family when they were in London was inexcusable. Instead she bombarded her daughter-in-law with long and effusively sanctimonious letters. The latter, to her credit, appears to have kept up a correspondence which must have tried her patience exceedingly. In this way Lady Frances learned of the successive births of Henry (who died six months later), Louisa, George, Selina, Henry Robert, Edmund Lewis, and Charles Hugh.

For the rest of his life the 'isolated Baronet' (as the headmaster of Repton School called him) lived in a self-imposed seclusion that in some respects is reminiscent of William Beckford's at Fonthill. Though he did not share Beckford's aversion to hunting he was fond of watching wildlife, and gave strict orders that hares and pheasants that bred within sight of his windows were to be allowed to feed undisturbed by keepers, dogs and cats. In the summer he and his wife went to places like Aberystwyth where the scenery was more interesting than the society. He had sold the house in Upper Grosvenor Street and was never seen in the drawing-rooms of the West End. But he adopted his father's practice of taking a substantial house in the Home Counties from which forays could be made to the shops and exhibitions of London without incurring the social obligations of a regular London residence. In the 1790s it was Stone House near Margate, from 1801 to 1805 Stourfield House near Christchurch in Hampshire. In 1808 he took Gatton Park in Surrey, and from 1812 to 1815 he had May Place near Dartford as well. In 1818 his choice fell on Mereworth Castle, but in the following year he removed to Barham House near Elstree in Hertfordshire.

Before he took a house Sir Henry had plans and elevations of it made for his inspection, and in 1816 alone his agents reported on at least twenty-five houses that were to let in the neighbourhood of London without finding one that pleased him. Wherever he lived, privacy was Sir Henry's first concern. At Stourfield it was understood locally that he took the house 'on account of its seclusion, as he was a very shy gentleman, and disliked meeting anyone, and seldom spoke when he did'. Here he had a private road built so that he could drive his carriage down to the beach without being seen.

At all these houses there was considerable expenditure on decoration and furniture, and Sir Henry's servants had a difficult time carrying out his capricious and exacting instructions. For Sir Henry was a man of sensibility and taste, and with an income of £10,000 a year, he could afford to have exactly what he wanted. At Calke in particular he could indulge in those improvements for which the varied terrain offered so much opportunity. The landscaping of the park had already been started by his father. Young Sir Henry continued the process of planting and earth-shifting which by the time of his death had transformed the old formal grounds into an outstanding picturesque landscape. A characteristic feature of the new layout was an underground tunnel which enabled gardeners and others to go about their business without intruding on the view from the east front of the house.

At the same time an elegant 'Casino' or Fishing Lodge was built at Swarkeston near the site of the old Harpur mansion. No trace of it now remains, but the accounts indicate that its interior included a Trellis Room, presumably one painted to simulate trellis-work, like the well-known room from Drakelow Hall, now

The Middle Lodge.

The Dining Room designed for Sir Henry Harpur by William Wilkins in 1793. The furniture in this room has been rearranged several times, and only the sideboard in the recess and some of the chairs appear to date from Sir Henry's time.

in the Victoria and Albert Museum. The Casino was designed by an architect called Samuel Browne, who carried out other works in the park at Calke and also helped Sir Henry to remodel the secondary family seat at Repton Park in the Gothic style. But Sir Henry's principal architect was not the obscure Browne, but the elder William Wilkins, who had just designed Donington Park for Sir Henry's neighbour Lord Moira. Donington is a Gothic extravaganza, but although Sir Henry decreed in 1808 that henceforth his house (known hitherto as 'Calke House', 'Calke Hall', or just as 'Calke') should be known as 'Calke Abbey', he made no attempt to Gothicise its architecture. What Wilkins was called upon to do was to give the entrance-front the conventional consequence of a portico, to create a new suite of principal rooms, including Drawing Room, Dining Room and Library, and to design lodges to mark the entrances to the park. How he accomplished his task, and how the new interiors were furnished is described on another page.

The Library was wholly new. Previous baronets had had but little use for books and no such room is mentioned in inventories of 1741 and 1748. But unlike his predecessors, Sir Henry was a man of intellectual interests and the contents of the library he collected bear out his mother's claim that he was a man of 'superior understanding and cultivated mind'. Architecture and music were well represented, and there was a sprinkling of law and military science. The legal and military books in Sir Henry's library were a recognition that in the reign of George III a great landowner, however much he might shrink from social contact, had inescapable public duties to perform. Thus Sir Henry was (at least nominally) on the Commission of the Peace, and in 1794 he was induced to serve his turn as Sheriff of Derbyshire (though 'how he would bear daylight' in that capacity excited some curiosity in the county).

In fact Sir Henry not only performed the usual ceremonial duties, but at the request of the Justices summoned a meeting of the gentlemen and yeomanry of Derbyshire 'for the consideration of the security of the Country'. England was then at war with Revolutionary France, and both invasion and civil disorder were

The title page of Haydn's 'Derbyshire Marches' commissioned by Sir Henry Harpur in 1794.

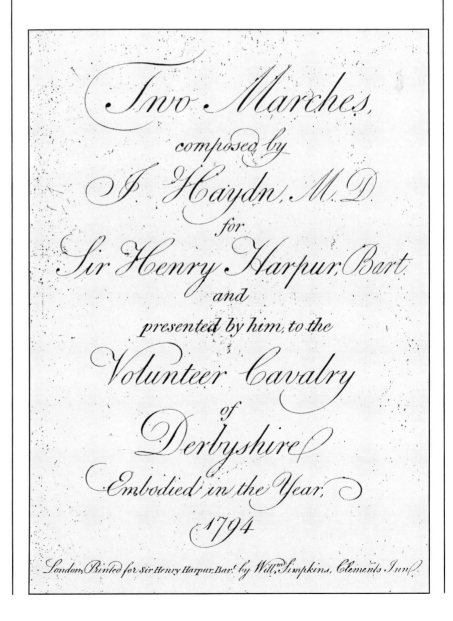

feared, especially by men of property. Eighty-four gentlemen agreed to subscribe to a fund 'in support of the Civil Power', the Duke of Devonshire and Sir Henry Harpur heading the list with £500 and £300 respectively. The result was the creation of the Derbyshire Volunteer Cavalry. It consisted of five troops, one of which was based on the Harpur estates. Sir Henry found himself 'Commanding Officer of the Calke or First Troop of Derbyshire Yeomanry Cavalry', with the rank of Captain and ultimately of Lieutenant Colonel. In 1804 there were 79 troopers under his command, with Sir Robert Wilmot of Osmaston as Lieutenant and Sir Henry's estate agent R. C. Greaves of Ingleby as Cornet. Most of the troopers were Sir Henry's own tenants. They were the successors of the county militias of the Armada years and the predecessors of the Home Guard of 1939–45. Having committed himself to this unwonted public duty, Sir Henry saw to it that the Calke Troop was equipped in suitable style. The troopers were issued with handsome blue uniforms adorned with the Harpur badge and crest, several examples of which are preserved in the house. In the Library there hangs a portrait of the black horse which Sir Henry rode at the head of his cavalry. It was painted by Clifton Tomson in 1810 and shows the horse accoutred for military service and held by Sir Henry's groom Stainsby.

But the *tour-de-force* of Sir Henry's military activities was the music to which his Troop marched. It was specially written for him by no less a musician than Josef Haydn, at that time perhaps the most celebrated composer in Europe. Haydn was then in London, and Sir Henry got his uncle Charles Greville to approach Haydn on his behalf. 'He has seen Haydn', reported Lady Frances, 'and spoken to him about your March. Charles desired he would make a charge, which at first he refused, and said he would leave it to you, but my brother told him when he acted by commission, he wished to be on a certainty. Haydn said he could compose a March in a short time, but a compleat composition in various parts, such as would do him credit, and gain approbation would take some time ... for such a March, including a Quick Step, he must name 24 guineas. As there is no bargaining with such eminent Composers, this is agreed upon. Charles desires me to add, as his own sentiments, that he wishes you to have it printed, and for you to present it, as the Derbyshire Volunteer Cavalry March, and to have it inserted, in the title, 'Composed by Haydn, and presented to the Derbyshire Cavalry by Sir Henry Harpur'. His reasons for this are; that it will be quite impossible for you to keep this March, merely for your Troop; the air of it, will be taken down, by those who hear it frequently, and a bad copy of it, made out. He thinks it will be a handsome and liberal present to the whole Corps and ... will always be called your March'. Charles Greville's advice was followed. The score was duly printed as *Two Marches composed by J. Haydn M.D. for Sir Henry Harpur Bart. and presented by him to the Volunteer Cavalry of Derbyshire embodied in the year 1794.* The engraved plates are preserved among the family archives, together with the original manuscript, partly in Haydn's own hand and partly in that of an amanuensis, with corrections by the composer.

The Yeomanry temporarily lifted Sir Henry out of his isolation and showed how his wealth and taste might have been employed in a wider sphere had his temperament allowed it. As it was, once the emergency was over, this 'sad shy creature' withdrew once more into his shell. Indeed his neurosis continued to grow. In 1812 the artist Joseph Farington was given a vivid account of the 'singularities' of the owner of Calke by some Leicestershire gentlemen who dined with him. 'At dinner', they said, 'he sits down alone at a table covered for several persons, and after dinner glasses are placed as if for company and he takes his wine in that form, but does not allow any servant to wait in the room. . . . He keeps a pack of hounds, but does not himself hunt, yet . . . he has pleasure in listening to his Huntsman while he gives an account of each chase. His shyness is a disease of the mind, which he is sensible of but cannot conquer, and in letters to his friends he laments that he labours under this difficulty. . . . He is shy of communication to such an excess that he sometimes delivers his orders to his servants *by letter.*' Some of these scribbled notes (mostly addressed to his Steward) actually survive to substantiate Farington's account.

Why a man who cared so little for society should have coveted a peerage is today difficult to understand. But in the reign of George III the equation between rank and hereditary wealth was still universally recognised. In Derbyshire the Harpurs were second only to the Cavendishes in acreage and wealth, yet the Cavendishes were dukes and the Harpurs were only baronets. It was in the hopes of attaining a rank commensurate with his wealth that Sir Henry

The Caricature Room is so called from the prints which are stuck onto its walls, all of them social caricatures by men such as Gillray and Cruickshank. Although print rooms were fashionable in the late eighteenth century, the display of caricatures rather than elegant decorative scenes and their haphazard arrangement on the walls make the Calke Caricature Room unique. As most of the prints date from the years 1798 to 1803, the room was probably created by Sir Henry Harpur (d. 1819), but some others found ready for use in a portfolio bear dates as late as 1825.

tried to get the dormant barony of Crewe of Steane revived in his favour. As his great-great-grandmother Catherine Crewe had been only one of the four co-heiresses of the last Lord Crewe of Steane (one other of whom besides herself had living male descendants) the prospect of success was remote. However, having hopefully changed his surname to Crewe in 1808, he petitioned Crown and Government for an honour which he had done little to earn by either public or political services. Inevitably it was in vain. But now the Crewe arms would be quartered with those of Harpur and the Crewe motto *Degeneranti genus opprobrium* ('To betray one's lineage is a disgrace') would take the place of the old *Cogita mori* which the Harpurs had acquired with the Findern estates in the sixteenth century. And in future the Crewe ancestry would be commemorated by the double surname of Harpur Crewe which has been borne by nearly all the subsequent owners of Calke to the present day.

On 6 February 1819 Sir Henry Crewe was driving a pair of young horses from Marylebone to the house he was then renting in Hertfordshire, where his wife and children were awaiting him for dinner. The horses became restive and one of the wheels of the carriage hit a post by the roadside. Sir Henry was thrown from his seat and fell on his head. Death was instantaneous. The funeral at

Silhouette portrait of the Rev. Henry Robert Crewe (1801–65) Rector of Breadsall, and his family, *circa* 1840.

Calke was reported in detail in the *Derby Mercury*, and may serve to illustrate the pomp with which members of the Harpur family, like other members of the landed aristocracy, were habitually interred in the eighteenth and nineteenth centuries.

> On Friday last the remains of the late Sir Henry Crewe were brought from his residence, Barham House, Herts., for interment at Calke Abbey. The funeral, which was as private as his rank would admit, was met at Loughborough and attended from there by the principal tenantry of the deceased; and on reaching the entrance of the Domain, about one o'clock, the procession was joined by the eldest sons of Sir Henry, the Bearers etc., and afterwards proceeded forward in the following order – Assistants etc. on horseback, the tenantry to the number of about 140 on horseback, two and two in deep mourning – with hatbands, gloves, and long black cloaks – Assistant carrying a superb board of feathers – the Hearse profusely ornamented with plumes of feathers, and decorated with escutcheons of the Arms of the deceased – drawn by six horses fully caparisoned and bearing plumes and escutcheons.

> Mourning coach drawn by six horses and containing Sir George Crewe Bart. and Henry Crewe Esqr., Chief Mourners – 2nd. Mourning Coach drawn by six horses and containing six clergymen friends of the deceased as pall bearers. 3rd Mourning Coach drawn by six horses containing the agents of Sir Henry and medical attendants. The family coach and four empty. The procession was closed by another carriage and four in which were the upper domestics of the family . . .

> On arriving at the Chapel the whole of the attendants dismounted and the tenantry lining the road on each side, the body followed by the mourners was borne through them into the Chapel. The Coffin was covered with rich crimson velvet, and superbly decorated with gold ornaments . . .

> The service was read by the Revd. Mr. Witt in the most impressive manner, during which the remains were deposited in the Vault among the illustrious ancestors of the family. The crowd of spectators assembled on this melancholy occasion was immense, and during the whole of the mournful ceremony, the utmost decorum and sympathy prevailed.

Sir George Crewe

Sir George Crewe was a young man of only 24 when he entered unexpectedly upon his inheritance in 1819. For his lifetime, the household at Calke was once more to be governed by the normal conventions of English upper-class life. An able and serious-minded man with a strong social conscience, he accepted his place in the affairs of the county, and devoted himself to fulfilling his duties as a Christian landlord and a country gentleman.

Between him and his father there was more than the usual generation gap. In his selfish isolation Sir Henry had been an eccentric example of a type of Georgian aristocrat who took his privileged position very much for granted. In Sir George, on the other hand, the new sense of social responsibility that was to be characteristic of the Victorian upper class was unusually highly developed. High moral standards, Christian charity and strict propriety were the principles that guided his conduct. Daily prayers and Sunday observance were the rule in his household. For him the ownership of a great estate was as much a responsibility as a source of pride, and for everything he considered himself to be accountable in the end to God.

That Sir George did not inherit these ideals from his father is obvious. His mother's initial lapse from virtue does not necessarily imply that she did not bring up her children in a responsible manner, but it was undoubtedly from his grandmother that Sir George derived the Evangelical piety that was the basis of his conduct. Before she was banned from Calke Lady Frances had already established a bond with her grandson which was immediately renewed after Sir Henry's death. Within a week of the fatal accident he had been to see her. 'This day, thank God (he confided to his diary) I once more was permitted to see my dear Grandmother. O Lord give me grace to profit by her excellent advice and example'. But for the change in moral climate that Sir George brought with him we must also look to his education at Rugby, then already a public school of national repute with a considerable and growing entry from the gentry. Here, in R. R. Bloxam's house, he was regarded as an exemplary pupil and he subsequently thought well enough of the school (of which he became a trustee) to send his own son there in due course.

The crisis following his father's death was a severe test of the young man's character. At the age of 24 he was suddenly called upon to administer an intestate estate (for Sir Henry had left no will), to reform a long mismanaged household, and to satisfy the claims of his widowed mother and of his younger brothers and sisters. From her house at Beckenham in Kent his grandmother bombarded him with well-meant but often ill-judged advice, while his mother made unreasonable demands on his time and generosity, asking for a house to be fitted up for her in the park at Calke and then rejecting it as soon as it was finished. His younger brother Henry, destined for the Church, wasted his time at Cambridge and showed signs of sharing his father's misanthropy, telling his grandmother that he 'was more averse than ever to any Society'. No wonder Sir George's family was in later years to remember 'how fearfully tried and harassed he was at this time'. His marriage in September gave him a partner with whom to share his responsibilities. Jane Whittaker came of a long line of East Anglian parsons. He had known her for some time and was now in a position to make her his wife without any need to seek parental consent.

At Calke Sir George proved to be a meticulous and exacting squire who found much to put right after his father's idiosyncratic regime. He tightened up the management both of his household and of his estates, and in 1838 was at last able to congratulate himself that 'under God's blessing, after 19 years' labours.... I have at last cleansed the Augaean stables of Calke jobs, Calke turkey and Calke extravagance'. One of many matters that demanded his

The Kitchen awaiting restoration after over forty years of disuse.

Sir George Crewe and his son John: from a portrait by R. R. Reinagle painted in 1828.

attention was the choice of a livery for his servants. As his father preferred to keep servants out of sight the wearing of a livery had evidently fallen out of use. Lady Frances advocated yellow, but this would not do, for as Sir George pointed out to her, in Derbyshire yellow happened to be the Radical colour. The livery eventually adopted (which Lady Frances thought 'too gaudy') was a green coat, with blue velvet collar and cuffs, and scarlet waistcoat and black plush breeches. Kitchen and Cellar were brought under control. Registers of every kind of consumption were instituted. In particular, a book was kept in which the name and purpose of every visitor to Calke was recorded day by day, together with the refreshment provided – an unique document in which the names of postmen, grooms, washerwomen and workmen are all written down, together with those of more exalted visitors coming to see Sir George himself on public or private business. His own life was equally strictly regulated. In 1820 he gave up hunting, not because he disapproved of it on principle, but because he regarded it as an indulgence for which he could no longer spare the time. And at the end of every day he searched his conscience and examined his conduct in an agony of Christian introspection.

As a landlord Sir George had the reputation of being both just and generous. When the publisher Sir Richard Phillips visited Calke in 1828 he praised the enlightened management of the estate. He heard 'many instances' of Sir George's 'acts of special generosity', and commented on the 'paternal spirit' which led him to provide over a thousand cottages for his poorer tenants, each with its garden-plot, which were let for nominal rents varying from 6d. to 5s. a year. The strong sense of social responsibility which activated Sir George is nowhere better illustrated than by his attention to his Staffordshire estate. As recently as 1796 the writer of a report on the agriculture of the county had remarked that 'to the eye of an intelligent ... stranger, familiar with a country highly cultivated', Staffordshire 'would convey the idea of a county just emerged, or emerging from barbarism'. This was particularly true of the remote moorlands where the Harpur estate lay. As Sir George himself observed, he was probably the first member of his family 'who ever set foot upon it, for any other purpose than shooting grouse'. At first he paid annual visits from Buxton, visits which soon convinced him that his Staffordshire tenants were '100 years behind the rest of the world, well disposed but ignorant and simple-minded'. Such day-visits were clearly not enough, and so in 1830 he built a 'small

The Entrance Hall made in 1841 and hung with the heads of remarkable cattle bred on the estate.

'A group of ponies in the park' by John Ferneley of Melton Mowbray, 1850. One of several paintings by this well-known animal painter acquired by Sir George Crewe and his son Sir John Harpur Crewe.

but convenient house' at Warslow, partly in order to house a resident agent and partly to provide accommodation for himself and his family. This was the house later known as 'Warslow Hall', and here he settled down for several weeks in the late summer of 1831, 'dispensing as far as possible with all the paraphernalia of either rank or wealth'.

From Warslow Sir George systematically explored his property and was appalled by what he found. 'When I first saw Quarnford, it appeared... the very end of the civilised world... the village of Flash was dirty, and bore marks specifically of Poverty, Sloth and Ignorance'. The clergy were little better than the peasants. One he found living with his half-naked children 'in a miserable cot by the mountain side', another was 'a constant occupier of the ale-house bench and of rough and uncouth manners', while the third was a clever man 'but of whose moral character there was no

good report'. The only doctor was a 'vulgar sot' who subsequently committed suicide. As for the farmers, they 'could not, in dress or appearance, be distinguished from my own day-labourers at Calke'.

Sir George saw it as his duty to bring moral and economic enlightenment to these backward and benighted people. To alleviate immediate want, blankets, great coats, flannel drawers and flannel waistcoats were distributed, and to celebrate the coronation of King William a dinner was given for the tenants at which Sir George, his agent and one of the clergy carved the meat. Soon arrangements were made for the church at Alstonfield and its chapels at Flash, Longnor and Warslow to be rebuilt or repaired, largely at Sir George's own expense. Schools and additional chapels were built in the outlying hamlets, and new parsonage houses were erected for occupation by worthier clergymen. Finally the whole area was transformed economically by the enclosure of over 3000 acres. The expense was considerable, and Sir George was not insensitive to the 'loss of the wild and picturesque character which the country formerly bore'. But the expenditure he regarded as a social duty, and he felt strongly that, in a time of rising population, 'no land which is capable of being cultivated, can be allowed to be idle for gratification to the eye'.

At Calke it was with 'a mixture of painful and pleasurable emotions' that Sir George had taken possession of his inheritance in 1819. 'This place looks so overwhelmingly large', he wrote in 1830, after an absence of some weeks. 'I cannot say its size makes me feel proud but rather to shrink within myself, in deep humility.' Nevertheless he subjected the house to a thorough repair, re-arranged the entrance hall, and gave the Saloon its finely moulded ceiling. He was also responsible for acquiring many of the pictures that now hang at Calke. Although his father had bought the four views of Naples by Ricciardelli that hang in the Breakfast Room, this seems to have been an isolated purchase by a man who spent more on architecture and gardening than he did on pictorial art. But Sir George, himself an amateur – though indifferent – painter in watercolours, was a regular purchaser of pictures. Some he bought at exhibitions, some he picked up at sales, and some he commissioned himself. The last were mostly scenes in Calke Park by John Glover and portraits of horses by James Ward and John Ferneley. As a collector his taste was for scenes from daily life rather than for 'history' painting, for British and Netherlandish artists rather than for Italian masters. In 1822/3 he purchased two of Landseer's earliest works, in 1826 one by John Linnell, and about the same time a 'Mother and Child' by William Etty. A Flemish 'Adoration of the Magi', 'Cows and Fishermen' attributed to Cuyp, an ice-scene by W. J. Müller, were characteristic purchases. One of his favourite acquisitions was a card-playing scene attributed to Jan Steen. It was not a particularly distinguished collection, but the choice was entirely his own, and it represented a shift in taste away from the sort of paintings traditionally favoured by the English aristocracy.

In public life Sir George Crewe was a man of strict principle who had no hesitation in doing whatever his conscience dictated, however contrary to established custom. Thus in 1821, as

Sheriff of the county, he discontinued the traditional Assize Ball, because he regarded it as unfeeling for ladies and gentlemen to amuse themselves in public at a time when others were lying in the condemned cell 'eking out the wretched remnant of their existence in all the most heart-rending agonies of mental distress'; and in 1827 he refused to subscribe to a plate for the Derbyshire Yeomanry to race for, because he considered that it would encourage betting. In 1831 he declared himself in favour of the Reform Bill, and proposed to offer himself for election to the new parliament. Derby was one of the towns where serious riots followed the rejection of the Bill, and the country houses of some of the Tory gentry were threatened by the mob. In this crisis Calke provided a refuge both for Sir Robert Wilmot-Horton of Osmaston and for Sir George's brother Henry, now rector of Breadsall.

When the Reform Bill was finally passed in March 1832 Sir George did not put himself forward, but in 1835, at a time when the Tory interest in Derbyshire 'was apparently lost without hope of recovery', he was persuaded to stand and won a notable victory at the polls. Such was his reputation as a man of principle that 'on the day of nomination at the county hall, when there was assembled a most ferocious mob yet under the influence of the Reform mania, when Sir George came forward there was a lull of the storm, and the worst speech that was addressed to him was when one of the mob called out good-humouredly, "Come, Sir George, give us a sermon"'. For six years he sat as one of the two Members for South Derbyshire. In the House of Commons he had the reputation of being almost 'too conscientious' for politics. Although he normally voted with the Conservatives (then in opposition under the leadership of Sir Robert Peel), he insisted that he 'went to parliament unshackled'. Thus he declined to vote against a Bill for the reform of Irish municipal corporations because he was satisfied that it would not (as his party alleged) harm the Church of Ireland. His reasons for voting in favour of a charter for London University were a nice blend of conservatism and liberalism. He did so, he said, because 'Dissenters were excluded from Oxford and Cambridge, and as it was not right to interfere with these Universities, it was but justice they should have one of their own'. Sir George rarely if ever spoke in the House, but he made his views on several issues known by means of printed pamphlets. In 1843 he drew on his personal knowledge to criticise the working of the Poor Law, and incidentally to condemn as a 'foul stain upon the name of Englishmen' the bastardy laws which 'visited upon the weaker sex, the sins of the stronger'. In 1830, under the pseudonym 'Agricola', he wrote a powerful indictment of the Game Laws, which he said he could no longer enforce as a magistrate.* Although the legalisation of the sale of game in 1831 met one of his main points, he told his son in 1843 that 'it would be quite as well for England if there were not a head [of game] in existence'.

Despite his piety and his principles Sir George Crewe was neither a prig nor a puritan. Although he brought the Assize Ball to

---

* The Game Laws gave the landed gentry the exclusive right to kill game of every sort and prohibited its sale. The penalties were severe.

Relics of the Battle of Trafalgar

Georgiana Lady Harpur Crewe was the daughter of a naval officer, Vice-Admiral William Stanhope Badcock (afterwards Lovell) (1788–1859), who took part in the Battle of Trafalgar on 21 October 1805. He was then a midshipman on the battleship *Neptune* (98 guns), which captured the Spanish flagship *Santissima Trinidada* (138 guns), then the largest ship afloat. The prize had to be scuttled, but Midshipman Badcock brought away with him an ornamental gilt dirk which belonged to the Spanish admiral's son, and this is preserved at Calke in a specially carved case. A letter from Badcock containing a vivid description of the battle is preserved among the Calke archives and was printed in the *English Historical Review* for 1890. At Calke there is also a painting of the battle by a naval artist, Lieut. R. S. Thomas, who illustrated Vice-Admiral Lovell's reminiscences, published in 1837. A portrait of the admiral's brother General Lovell Benjamin Lovell (1786–1861), another hero of the Napoleonic Wars, hangs on the stairs.

an end, he and Lady Crewe gave the County a handsome enough entertainment on another occasion, and at Calke a floor (presumably that of the Saloon) was chalked for dancing on at least one occasion. When two maids were found to be pregnant, Sir George drily noted in one of his memoranda books:

2 Mishaps in the Calke Family

Offender – on one side

Samuel Williams	Footman to me
James Baxter	Coachman to Dowager Lady Crewe

Per Contra

Sarah Taylor	Lady's maid to Lady Crewe
Anne Walker	Do to Dowager Lady Crewe

Like his father, Sir George was slight in build (at the age of 30 he weighed only 8 stone 2 lb.) and his health was never good. Neuralgia afflicted his legs and he suffered from chronic bronchitis. It was from a severe attack of bronchitis that he died on 1 January 1844. Thus, as his agent noted in his diary, 'there was lost to his friends and dependants the most kind and benevolent man that ever lived in his 49 years'. He left three sons and four daughters. With the exception of his eldest son, none of them married. The two younger sons, Evelyn and Richard, both obtained commissions in the Dragoon Guards and served in the Army for the rest of their active lives. Of the daughters only two were in any way remarkable, Mary Adeline for longevity (she died in 1930, aged 95) and Isabel Jane (d.1909) for the collections she made for a family history.

The Last Two Baronets

From 1819 to 1844 Calke Abbey came near to realising the ideal of the English country house as a social, political and economic entity. With an ample income derived from an intelligent exploitation of a large estate, an enlightened owner lived among his tenants, acted as a leading figure in county affairs, and took his place in the national legislature at Westminster. The great house was the centre of a little world whose affairs were largely decided within its walls by the man who was both owner of the land, patron of the livings, Justice of the Peace, Commanding Officer of the Yeomanry, and a member of innumerable boards and committees ranging from the management of the County Infirmary to the administration of the Poor Law. He appointed the clergy, built the schools, licensed the public houses and provided employment for many of the inhabitants of Calke and Ticknall. He was well known to everyone in the neighbourhood, often visited them in their homes, and was always ready to listen to their difficulties and to help those who were in need. His benevolence was almost as systematic and certainly more humane than that of the modern welfare state.

The household at Calke was, of course, far from self-sufficient. But it baked its own bread, brewed its own beer, had its own dairy, and from time to time killed its own mutton. The deer in the park, though kept more for prestige than for food, provided venison in season, and enabled the owner to send complimentary haunches to friends and relations. Only in the wine-cellar were the

Abraham Fairbrother, Gamekeeper at Calke since the 1830s, photographed about thirty years later.

products of foreign countries much in evidence. As for building materials, stone, brick and lime were all available on the estate. England was, in any case, the workshop of the world, and if brass locks, iron railings or other metal goods were required, they could be obtained from no farther afield than Derby, Belper, Birmingham or Wolverhampton.

This picture of a country house community is one whose attractions can easily be exaggerated: it depended too much on the vigilance and commitment of one man to retain its quality indefinitely, and in any case social, political and economic changes were gradually to destroy it. At Calke the decline had already begun in the 1850s, not so much because of external pressures as because Sir John Harpur Crewe did not choose to claim the position in society to which he was entitled. He lacked the moral compulsion which had so powerfully motivated his father. An education at Rugby and Trinity College, Cambridge, failed to stimulate a sluggish intellect, and a natural diffidence prevented him from playing any part in politics or from taking any initiative in county affairs. The daily routine of a great estate was enough to occupy his time. His father had foreseen the danger. 'I should not like to see my son inferior in information to those of his own rank and class', wrote Sir George in an admonitory letter in 1843, 'my only anxiety . . . is if I see the whole day consumed in out-of-door amusement, which

Facing page: Sir John Harpur Crewe, the owner of Calke from 1844 to 1886.

Illuminated address presented by the Derbyshire tenants to Richard Harpur Crewe when he attained his majority in 1901. The text is surrounded by views of places on the estate.

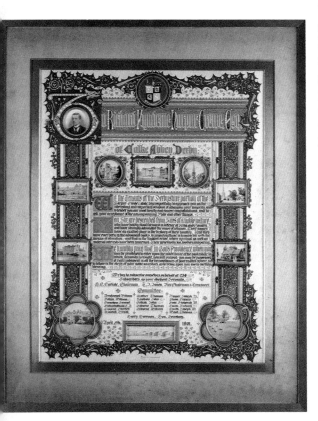

prevents the possibility of giving the mind any food on that day'. Out-of-door amusement was, however, just what most appealed to Sir John. At Calke his great interest was the breeding of longhorn cattle and Portland sheep. The prizes that they won at agricultural shows were the only recognition that he sought, and although he served his turn as High Sheriff in 1853 (when his 'long procession of tenantry, all mounted on good horses with new harness ... made quite a sensation in the borough of Derby') little was seen of him outside his own property. For Sir John, as the epitaph on his monument declares, 'was averse to a public life and spent the greater part of his days at Calke amongst his own people in the exercise of unostentatious charity'. The Harpur-Crewe estate might be the second largest in Derbyshire, but the house had never been a show-place like Chatsworth or Kedleston, and outside the neighbourhood few knew of its existence. It had never figured in books like Neale's *Seats*, and although Sir Bernard Burke did devote a column or two to it in his *Visitations of Seats and Arms* of 1852, it is significant that it does not appear on a map of 'the Great Landowners of England and Wales' published in 1865 – a map which includes, besides Chatsworth and Kedleston, almost all the other great houses in Derbyshire.

Animals, tame or wild, living or dead, were now becoming Calke's principal *raison d'être*. In the park the longhorn cattle and the Portland sheep shared the herbage with the two herds of deer. Inside the house the entrance hall was hung with the mounted heads of prize oxen. Upstairs the cult of the horse was celebrated by more paintings by John Ferneley, including the huge 'Council of Horses', in which the artist attempted to give a group of animals the dignity of a mythological subject. At Warslow the house built by Sir George as a base from which to civilise the moorlands became a shooting-box. From 1845 onwards the game-books show a steady increase in the number of partridges and pheasants killed, an increase which was matched by the intensified slaughter of their predators. A tally of 'vermin' killed on the Staffordshire estate between 1860 and 1880 lists 5701 cats, 2256 stoats, 2073 weasels, 1784 magpies, 974 crows, 733 hawks, 23 foxes and 9 polecats. In 1838 there had been four gamekeepers on Sir George's payroll; by the 1870s there were ten on Sir John's.

On the estate the sense of paternalist obligation on the one hand and of loyal deference on the other was still very real and very strong. When Sir John's eldest son Vauncey came of age in 1867 the tenantry were entertained at a series of dinners, and illuminated addresses were presented, not only from every part of the estate, but also from the inhabitants of Ashby, Melbourne and Derby, towns in which there was no Harpur property but an abundance of goodwill towards a rich and generous neighbour to whose benevolence speaker after speaker testified. In 1876 Vauncey's marriage was the occasion for another display of territorial loyalty. He and his bride (the daughter of the Tory statesman Charles Bowyer Adderley, later Lord Norton) arrived by train from Derby and were driven to Calke by way of Chellaston, Swarkeston, Stanton, Melbourne and Ticknall, at each of which

Sir Vauncey Harpur Crewe as a child.

places they were greeted by flowers, flags and triumphal arches of evergreen (see p. 97).

But life at Calke was not quite as glamorous as these state occasions might suggest. For the Abbey was once more the home of a man who cared little for the society of his neighbours. In her journal Lady Harpur Crewe lamented the social isolation to which she was condemned. 'I wish', she wrote plaintively on New Year's Day 1857, 'I might be allowed to do more like other people, and have a few friends sometimes, it would cheer me and do me good'. But for her there was no question of the fashionable house-parties of late Victorian England. Plans made by Decimus Burton's nephew Henry Marley Burton in 1867 for various improvements, including a new sitting-room on the west side of the house communicating with a conservatory, came to nothing. All that Lady Harpur Crewe was able to achieve was the redecoration and rearrangement in 1856 of the Drawing Room, though even here some of the late Georgian furniture remained under the Victorian loose-covers. The fossilisation of Calke had begun.

Sir John Harpur Crewe died in March 1886, after 42 years as the owner of Calke. He had married in 1845 his cousin Georgiana, daughter of Vice-Admiral William Stanhope Lovell, by Selina, daughter of his grandfather Sir Henry Crewe. They had three children, Vauncey (so named after a remote medieval ancestor of the Crewes), Hugo and Alice. To judge by an early photograph Vauncey was a delicate child, and he was educated privately at Calke, attending neither public school nor university. He was, however, brought up to observe the natural life in which the park at Calke was rich, and at the age of twelve wrote the first volume of a 'Natural History of Calke and Warslow', in which he listed nearly a hundred species of birds that he and his father had identified in the park or on the ponds at Calke, ranging from a pair of golden eagles to numerous varieties of geese and ducks. A second volume in which he intended not only to deal with the botany and conchology of Calke but also to set down 'my grievances and amuseing occurrances of every day life' has, alas, not been found.

Birds, alive, dead, but above all stuffed, were to be the dominant interest in Sir Vauncey's life. From Sir Henry (d. 1819) onwards, every owner of Calke had been something of an ornithologist. As early as 1793 the accounts record payments for preserving or 'naturalising' birds. By 1840 there were already nearly two hundred cases of stuffed birds, quadrupeds and fishes at Calke. Many of these belonged to Sir George's eldest son, who added to their number after he had inherited the property and who also made the collection of minerals and fossils that is still to be seen in the Saloon and elsewhere in the house. But what for his predecessor had been a pastime became for Sir Vauncey an all-absorbing passion, upon which he regularly spent a substantial amount of money. Although as a young man he went on an ornithological visit to Egypt, his collection was almost entirely of British birds, or rather of birds found in the British Isles, since it included many rare migrants. Some were shot by Sir Vauncey himself, who was rarely seen without a gun on his shoulder, but many were purchased from dealers and correspondents all over the country, and many were bought at auction in Stevens's rooms in King Street, Covent Garden. It was here in 1894 that Sir Vauncey paid 300 guineas for the Great Auk's egg that was the pride of his collection.

Although Sir Vauncey was a member of the British Ornithologists' Union and bought many books about birds and lepidoptera (which he also collected on a large scale), his interest in these subjects was scarcely scientific. For him bird-watching, shooting and collecting were complementary activities. It was Natural History of a fairly elementary kind, in which the predominant motives were those of the hunter and the hoarder rather than of the classifier or the scientific observer. The park at Calke was his private game reserve, while year by year the house came to look more and more like a museum. By the time of his death in 1924 the number of specimens amounted to several thousands, and the glass cases had invaded every floor of the house. With the exception of Lord Rothschild's at Tring, it may have been the largest private collection of its sort in the country, though certainly the least known.

For Sir Vauncey was a recluse for whom his house and park were a sanctuary from society. Apart from serving as High Sheriff of Derbyshire in 1900 he played absolutely no part in public life. By the 1890s, it is true, the newly-established County Councils were taking over from the gentry many of the functions which had hitherto been the latter's prerogative. But a great landowner still had a place in local society – even in the County Council – if he chose to claim it. For Sir Vauncey such activities had no attraction: his was not a retreat in the face of superior forces, it was a voluntary abdication. 'How completely he is losing or rather has lost all position in the County', lamented his aunt Isabel in 1904. 'It vexes me terribly, I can't understand him. He does not seem to know how to behave like a gentleman'. It was Sir Henry all over again – and Sir Henry was, after all, his great-grandfather on both sides. There was the same unsociability, the same sometimes arbitrary behaviour, and the same 'shyness of communication'. At least during the latter part of his life, he had little to do with his wife and children. He and Lady Harpur Crewe led separate lives. When she entertained visitors he made off into the woods, setting his coachman to keep watch and tell him when the intruders had departed. Only then would he come out of cover and return to the house. His only confidant was his head gamekeeper Agathos Pegg, who regularly accompanied him on shooting and butterflying expeditions. With the other servants he was on such distant terms that, like Sir Henry, he often communicated with them only by letter, especially if he was dissatisfied with their conduct. A frequent source of complaint was the management of the fires which he kept burning in order to maintain his specimens at an even temperature. If a fire was found to be either too hot or not hot enough, a written message would be sent by a footman ordering the instant dismissal of the offender. As Sir Vauncey scarcely knew one maid or under-footman from another these orders were generally ignored, and some servants survived two or three sackings without the evasion being realised by their irascible employer.

Sir Vauncey Harpur Crewe in old age.

Part of Sir Vauncey's huge collection of lepidoptera and birds' eggs.

Sir Vauncey's arbitrary conduct was an hereditary trait which went back even further than his great-grandfather. For long ago in the eighteenth century Sir Robert Burdett, who had married the widow of the fifth baronet in 1753, used to say of the Harpurs, 'Sir, there is no dependence upon [them], they are a capricious, uncertain race'. Sometimes these outbursts had serious consequences. One summer's day in the 1890s Sir Vauncey decided to go butterflying at Repton Park with his gamekeeper Pegg. Repton Park (p. 90) was a small country house on the estate which Sir Henry had remodelled in a picturesque style, adding battlemented turrets to the existing rectangular structure. It had been occupied, first by Sir Henry's third son Edmund Lewis, and then, after the latter's death in 1874, by his son John Edmund Harpur Crewe. Sir Vauncey was not on good terms with his cousin, and his unannounced appearance on the latter's lawn with his butterfly nets led to an altercation. Sir Vauncey immediately returned to Calke, sent for his agent, and ordered him to pull the house down. Within a week Repton Park had been demolished, leaving the unfortunate occupant to find a new home at his own expense in the neighbouring village of Milton.

Another victim of Sir Vauncey's anger was his daughter Airmyne, with whom his relations were so bad that he sometimes

The Bird Lobby, with its display of stuffed birds collected by Sir Vauncey.

communicated with her through the public post. One of his obsessions was the fear of fire. Smoking was strictly forbidden throughout the house. But Sir Vauncey suspected Airmyne of smoking in the seclusion of her room, and set Pegg to keep a watch on her. Pegg found that his employer's suspicions were well founded but decided not to give her away. One warm evening, however, cigarette smoke drifted through her open window into Sir Vauncey's on the storey above. He came down, caught her red-handed, and ordered her to leave Calke immediately. She had to spend the night in Derby, and was never allowed back during her father's lifetime.

Yet the traditional solicitude for the tenants on the estate persisted, and to a visiting workman at least, the regime at Calke could seem unusually benevolent. In 1888 a man who had been sent by the sculptor Boehm to set up the monument to Sir John Harpur Crewe in Calke Church felt impelled to write to Sir Vauncey to thank him 'for the great kindness' he had shown to him and his mate. 'If all the well to do', he concluded, 'were to treat those that work for them, as well as you do, there would not be that bitter feeling between the classes that there now is'.

However arbitrary his conduct may have been to his daughters, Sir Vauncey appears always to have been on good terms

To run Calke Abbey required a staff of 20 to 30 servants. The number fluctuated, but there were 25 in 1737 and, as this photograph shows, 27 in about 1910. The head servants were the cook, the butler, the housekeeper and the chief housemaid, here shown seated amid their subordinates. Under the housekeeper came the housemaids, nurserymaids, laundrymaids and footmen, while the kitchenmaids and scullerymaids took their orders from the cook. Life 'below stairs' was quite as hierarchical as it was above. With the exception of the cook and her staff, who ate in the Kitchen, all the other servants had their meals in the Servants' Hall. The ritual here was formidable. A footman held the door open for the housekeeper, the butler and the ladies' maids. These superior servants ate their first course in the Hall with the others, and then retired to the Housekeeper's Room, where they had their sweet. The lower servants (who had a sweet only three days a week) were not allowed to speak until they had gone. In the group above the two footmen stand at either side, while the three ladies' maids are seated on the ground in front.

with his son Richard, allowing him the means to indulge in a fondness for travel, ships, motoring, aeroplanes and other manifestations of modern life that were rigorously excluded from the precincts of Calke, within which neither motor-car nor bicycle was allowed in Sir Vauncey's lifetime. The ban did not, however, extend to Ticknall, and there Richard kept a car in which Sir Vauncey would sometimes allow himself to be driven to Warslow. At Calke Richard was permitted to operate a small hand printing press upon which he printed programmes for the theatrical performances which he and his sisters were in the habit of giving in the 1890s. From 1905 onwards he had an income of his own from the Hemington estate (left to his uncle Hugo by Sir John and by Hugo bequeathed to himself) and spent most of his time in Hampshire or London, away from the oppressive atmosphere of Calke. For a year or two he acted as private secretary to the Conservative politician R. W. Hanbury, M.P. for North Staffordshire and President of the Board of Agriculture in Lord Salisbury's government, but Hanbury's death in 1903 meant the end of this brief venture into public life.

Had Richard Harpur Crewe lived to succeed his father, Calke would have come to terms with the twentieth century after Sir Vauncey's death in 1924, but his health was never good and he predeceased his father, dying of cancer in 1921. The estate then passed to his eldest sister Hilda. Hilda had married Colonel Godfrey Mosley, a member of the gentry (he was the second son of the Rev. Rowland Mosley of Burnaston House near Derby) and a partner in the firm of Derby solicitors (Taylor, Simpson and Mosley) who

acted for the Calke estate. To help to pay the Death Duties the Mosleys sold off a considerable quantity of stuffed birds, eggs and lepidoptera, as well as some of the most valuable books such as Audubon's *Birds of America* and Gould's *Birds of Australia*. They were obliged to reduce their establishment from about twenty-seven servants to a mere half-dozen, motor-cars were no longer banned, and a telephone was installed. But in every other respect Hilda and her husband maintained Calke exactly as it had been in her father's lifetime. When she died in 1949, Calke went to her nephew Charles Jenney, the elder son of her younger sister Frances and her husband Arthur Jenney.

In Charles Harpur-Crewe (he changed his name in 1961, when he served as High Sheriff) the Harpur heredity asserted itself once more. He was educated at Bedford School and then joined the Army. As a junior officer in the Sherwood Foresters he reached Singapore just in time to witness its fall. His subsequent experiences as a fugitive in the Malayan jungle may well have played a part in forming an awkward personality in which there still lurked traces both of that arbitrary behaviour remarked upon by Sir Robert Burdett, and of that secretiveness which had made recluses of Sir Henry (d.1819) and Sir Vauncey. His agents found him a difficult

Richard Harpur Crewe, Sir Vauncey's only son, died in 1921 before he could inherit the house and title. Unlike his father he was a keen motorist and loved ships, aeroplanes and other modern inventions.

Charles Harpur-Crewe dressed as High Sheriff of Derbyshire in 1961, flanked by his Chaplain (the Rev. C. H. Cave) and his Solicitor (Mr. J. R. S. Grimwood-Taylor).

man to serve and he consorted little with other Derbyshire land-owners, preferring the company of tenant farmers, with whom he talked in their own Midland accent rather than in that of the upper classes. Except in the year of his shrievalty (when there was a dinner party for the gentry, and a garden-party for the tenantry) he lived alone in almost total seclusion. For in Charles Harpur-Crewe's time Calke was still a house which never opened its doors, not merely to the public, still less to the cognoscenti, but even to local county society. Outside Calke he played a limited part in public life as a governor of Repton School, a member of the South Derbyshire District Council, and as Chairman of the local Conservative Party. But he rarely spoke and made little contribution to the meetings he attended. He died suddenly in March 1981, while engaged in setting mole-traps in the park.

4 CALKE GOES PUBLIC

Victorian toy soldiers.

WHEN, IN March 1981, the Harpur-Crewe estate passed to Charles's younger brother Henry, the spell that had bound Calke for so long was at last broken. The new owner was ready to seek advice from those qualified to give it, and to welcome visitors with suitable credentials. To those who penetrated its rooms for the first time it was evident that what in the nineteenth century had been a social anomaly, and in the early twentieth an eccentric anachronism, had by the present decade become a unique

historical document. For thanks to the aversion of its previous owners to social intercourse, Calke was a house that in almost every essential had remained quite unchanged for over a hundred years. Victorian photographs testified that the state rooms were furnished and arranged precisely as they were at the death of Sir John Harpur Crewe. The Drawing Room, in particular, faithfully preserved, in its stuffy congestion of chairs, sofas and occasional tables, the authentic clutter of the 1860s and 1870s. Nowhere else in England could the atmosphere of a Victorian drawing room be experienced quite as it could at Calke, where every picture, every piece of furniture, and almost every individual ornament, remained exactly where it was in 1886.

In the Saloon, the beautiful portrait by Tilly Kettle of Lady Frances Harpur and her infant son still hung over the chimneypiece, looking down on the same array of stuffed birds, fossils, specimen minerals, polished stones and miscellaneous antiquities as it did in the 1880s. Upstairs, in the bedrooms, and downstairs, in the kitchen area, disorder prevailed, but in almost every room there was something either of intrinsic value or of historic interest to discover. In one the component parts of a magnificent Georgian State Bed, its silk hangings in pristine condition, remained undisturbed in the great chest in which they were sent down from London two hundred or more years ago. In others investigation disclosed military uniforms of the Napoleonic era, relics of the Battle of Trafalgar, the notebooks of a famous Egyptologist, Victorian children's toys, and, in the Muniment Room, the records of a great estate from the twelfth century to the twentieth. Outside, in the stables, the tackroom was still redolent of the age of the horse, while the smithy and the joiner's shop were potentially working museums of their respective crafts. With its magnificent park (enhanced rather than impaired by the reservoir which in 1956–8 drowned some of its eastern perimeter), its considerable architectural interest and its unique contents, Calke was one of those entities for whose preservation public policy had striven for the last thirty years. Situated within twenty miles of Nottingham, Derby, Leicester and Burton-on-Trent, its recreative potentialities were as obvious as its value as an outstanding visual relic of the past.

But in 1981 Calke Abbey lay under the threat of a second dissolution. In the maze of fiscal penalties and concessions created by the modern state to redistribute wealth on the one hand while seeking on the other to preserve some of the cultural heritage created by that wealth in the past, great houses and great estates survive only with the aid of the best legal and financial expertise. Not only did Charles Harpur-Crewe fail to seek that expertise: he appears to have given no thought at all to the future of Calke. He did not even trouble to make a will. However, the devolution of the property of which he was the owner for life depended not on any will that he might have made but on the trust created by his aunt Hilda Mosley in 1940. Mrs. Mosley and her nephew were not on good terms, and this may help to explain the way the trust was framed: it was a 'strict settlement' of a kind which left very little room for manoeuvre in any event, and virtually none in the circum-

The Saddle-room in the stables, still redolent of the age of the horse.

stances which arose in 1981. Charles died unmarried, and after him the property would go first to his brother Henry and then to his sister Airmyne, both of whom were also unmarried. In the absence of any other known heirs no steps could have been taken in Charles's lifetime either to bar the entail or to short-circuit the inheritance in such a way as to avoid three successive tranches of Capital Transfer Tax. So far as the house was concerned some sort of charitable foundation might have been devised to maintain it in perpetuity free of CTT, and after 1975 a Maintenance Fund could have been set up, though until the 1980 Finance Act that expedient had too many built-in disadvantages to recommend it, and Charles's death followed the 1980 Act too closely to allow time for action even had he been aware of its provisions. It was, however, even more unfortunate that he did not live a few days longer, for then the estate would automatically have benefited substantially from certain provisions in the 1981 Act reducing the incidence of CTT on lands not in hand.

So in 1981 Henry Harpur-Crewe found himself the owner for life of an estate worth some £14m., on which the liability

Victorian dolls found undisturbed in
a chest of drawers.

Childrens' toys in the School Room.

for CTT amounted to nearly £10m. Three options presented themselves: to sell everything, pay the tax, and enjoy the still substantial residue; to sell land and chattels to the necessary value, obtain exemption from CTT on the house and park and continue to live there for the rest of his life; or to surrender the house and contents in lieu of tax and thus ensure its preservation as an historic building in the care of some body such as The National Trust. For a young man with a family the first might well have been the appropriate course of action, but for a bachelor in his sixties with financial resources of his own it seemed unnecessarily drastic. The second would have had its attractions had the house been in good structural order, but it was doubtful whether the income from the reduced estate would be sufficient to carry out the extensive repairs that would be necessary, and it was obvious that, even if Calke could precariously survive for Henry's lifetime, the end would come when further tax became due on his death. In fact it was clear that Calke could be saved only if house and contents could be accepted in lieu of tax. To this course Mr. Harpur-Crewe readily agreed, as his overriding wish was to ensure the preservation of Calke after his death. So house, contents and almost the entire estate up to the value of the tax owed were offered to the Treasury in the hope that in the hands of The National Trust the revenue from the estate would provide the necessary funds for repair and maintenance. After an inordinate delay the Treasury agreed to accept house, contents and park (together valued at upwards of £2m.) but refused the 'non-heritage' land which supported them. It looked as if Calke was doomed by the unwillingness of the Treasury to find any way which would enable the preservation of the house to be balanced against the enormous sum to be received in CTT. Here was a house that everyone agreed should be kept for posterity, whose owner was anxious to surrender it to a Trust willing to accept it, yet was prevented from doing so by the very government which ought to have been doing its best to facilitate the transaction.

Calke, it seemed, would follow Mentmore as a cultural bargain which the government was determined to refuse. But by 1981 Conservation had become a national preoccupation, almost a political force. Within the 'establishment', the National Heritage Memorial Fund, the Historic Buildings Council, the Parliamentary Heritage Group, and The National Trust itself, all urged the government to think again, while outside it every newspaper and every television company featured the plight of the 'time-capsule house'. At Calke Henry Harpur-Crewe amiably tolerated the invasion of innumerable reporters, television crews, members of Parliament and others, and allowed himself to be filmed and photographed rummaging among the antique debris of his family home. *Country Life* provided some informed articles about Calke and its history, while glossy magazines offered beautifully atmospheric photographs of a great house in deliciously picturesque decay. SAVE distributed an urgent and compelling leaflet and a perfectly-chosen poster that was widely displayed. *The Times*, in the course of an eloquent leader entitled 'A Little Piece of England', pointed out that the physical fossilisation which made Calke unique and the failure to master the arts of tax avoidance were closely linked: in acknowledging the one, the government must make allowance for the other. Meanwhile the interest on the unpaid tax continued to mount at the rate of £1300 a day. By the spring of 1984 the total tax bill amounted to over £11¼m. It was obvious that sales could not be delayed any longer, and that they might have to include land and works of art essential to Calke's integrity as an historic entity. In this extremity the Heritage Fund took the initiative by bringing together all the interests concerned: could a package be devised? The National Trust, with the aid of an anonymous benefactor, undertook to contribute £1m., while the Harpur-Crewe Trustees offered a like amount. The Department of the Environment indicated its willingness to help by reconsidering the amount of land adjoining the park that might be deemed to be of 'heritage quality'. But the gap between the amount of money· promised and that needed to ensure the future of the house was too great to be filled by anyone but the government itself. Would the government relent? The answer came dramatically in the Budget Speech on 13 March. The Chancellor of the Exchequer, Mr. Nigel Lawson, announced that he would provide the National Heritage Memorial fund with £4·5m. to save Calke Abbey. It was the first time that the claims of conservation and the heritage had been formally recognised in a Budget Speech. Thanks to SAVE and the media, to the pressure exerted inside and outside Parliament, above all to the persistence of Arthur Alexander, the lawyer acting on behalf of Henry Harpur-Crewe and his trustees, the campaign for Calke Abbey had ended in an outstanding victory for the conservation movement.

Sir Gardner Wilkinson

Sir Gardner Wilkinson (1797–1875), whose portrait by H. W. Phillips is reproduced opposite, was a great nineteenth-century antiquary and archaeologist who ranks as the father of British Egyptology. He spent many years in Egypt from 1821 onwards, studying and surveying the monuments and transcribing hieroglyphic inscriptions. He published several works on the subject, including *A Topographical Survey of Thebes* (1826) and *Manners and Customs of the Ancient Egyptians* (1837). Although it was as an Egyptologist that he made his reputation, Wilkinson was also interested in classical and prehistoric archaeology and made thousands of beautiful and accurate drawings of antiquities all over Europe and the eastern Mediterranean. The picture above is his drawing of an Etruscan tomb at Cerveteri in Italy, of which it is an important record.

Wilkinson was a cousin of Georgiana Lady Harpur Crewe, and when he died in 1875 he left his library, his sketch-books and all his manuscript notes to Sir John Harpur Crewe to be preserved as an heirloom. This valuable collection has passed to The National Trust with the house and the manuscripts and sketch-books have been deposited in the Bodleian Library at Oxford for the use of scholars. Wilkinson was also an amateur woodcarver, and left all his carvings to Sir John. Two cabinets with panels carved by him are placed near the top of the stairs, and another specimen of his workmanship can be seen in the Entrance Hall. It was a chimneypiece in one of the rooms in his house at Brynfield in Glamorganshire and was converted by Sir John into a china cabinet (right).

5 THE ESTATE

A COUNTRY HOUSE like Calke Abbey was more than just a luxurious home: it was the symbol of a family dynasty and the focus of a great estate. All over England, from the sixteenth century to the nineteenth, it was taken for granted that the continuity of such a family and the preservation of its estate transcended the personal interest of any individual member. Each successive owner regarded himself as bound to hand on both his name and his property to his heir, and if he showed any disposition to neglect that duty, then he would find that the family lawyers had limited his freedom of action by the legal device known as the strict settlement. Such settlements were usually made afresh when the eldest son married, and they not only made financial provision for his widow and his younger children, but laid down the order of succession among his heirs and restrained both him and them from doing anything that might diminish the capital value of the estate, for instance by selling land or leasing it for a long period. For his lifetime he had unfettered enjoyment of the income, but the estate itself he could not touch. It was by a series of such settlements that the descent of the Harpur patrimony was regulated. It was, for instance, in accordance with one of them, drawn up in 1670, that the main Harpur lands passed to the Calke branch of the family in 1679, and it was another, made in 1940, whose unduly inflexible terms were partly responsible for the downfall of the estate in 1981.

The estate, consisting of land, was something whose integrity and continuity could be secured by lawyers and other professional advisers. It was, of course, liable to taxation, and it was subject to the sometimes arbitrary powers exercised by the state. As Royalists the Harpurs experienced those powers during the Commonwealth, but not to a degree that seriously impaired their inheritance. After the political revolution of 1688 property was safe, and for the next two centuries parliamentary taxation was never a crushing burden on a great estate such as Calke. But in the present century Income Tax, Surtax, Death Duties and finally Capital Transfer Tax have reached proportions that are deliberately de-

The Harpur-Crewe Estate in Derbyshire and Leicestershire. Places where the Harpur family owned land are named in bolder lettering. The line of the tramway which carried lime from the Ticknall lime-kilns to the Ashby-de-la-Zouch Canal is shown.

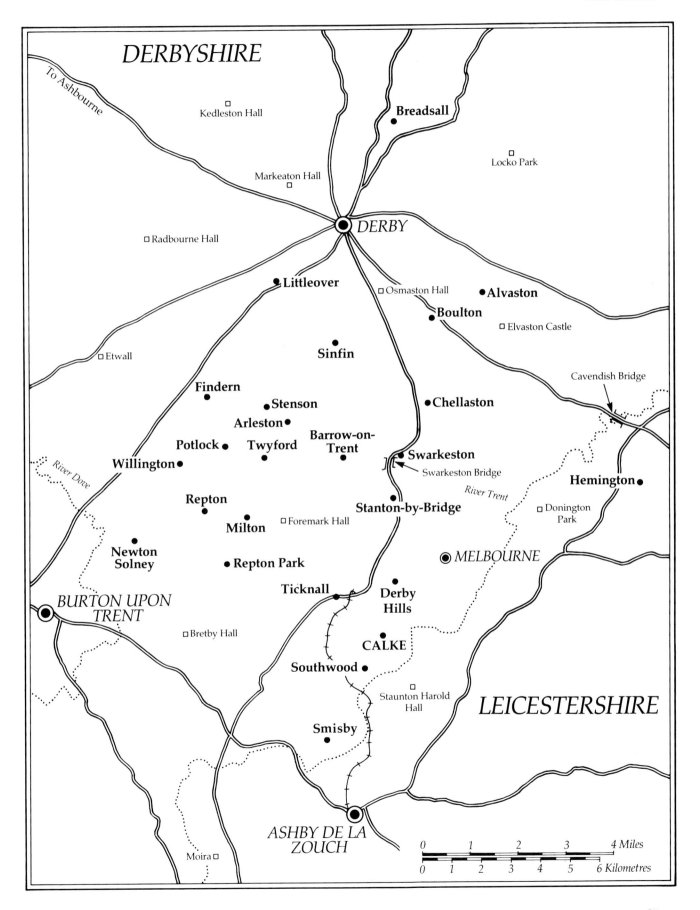

DERBYSHIRE

To Ashbourne

Kedleston Hall

Breadsall

Locko Park

Markeaton Hall

⬤ *DERBY*

□ Radbourne Hall

Littleover

□ Osmaston Hall

Alvaston

Boulton

□ Elvaston Castle

□ Etwall

Sinfin

Cavendish Bridge

Findern

Stenson

Chellaston

Arleston

Barrow-on-Trent

Potlock   **Twyford**

Willington

Swarkeston

Swarkeston Bridge

River Dove

Hemington

River Trent

Repton

□ Foremark Hall

Stanton-by-Bridge

□ Donington Park

Milton

Newton Solney

Repton Park

⬤ *MELBOURNE*

BURTON UPON TRENT

Ticknall

Derby Hills

□ Bretby Hall

CALKE

Southwood

Staunton Harold Hall

LEICESTERSHIRE

Smisby

ASHBY DE LA ZOUCH

Moira □

| 0 | 1 | 2 | 3 | 4 Miles |

| 0 | 1 | 2 | 3 | 4 | 5 | 6 Kilometres |

The end of the tunnel which carried the tramway under the drive on its way to the lime-kilns.

signed to break down great accumulations of inherited wealth, and of this confiscatory policy (pursued by Labour and Tory governments alike) the Harpur-Crewe estate has been a notable victim.

The continuity of the family, on the other hand, was much more difficult to ensure, for it depended on the accidents of birth and death. No human device could guarantee that son would succeed father in unbroken succession for generation after generation. Either there would be no male heir or the son would die before the father – the latter a calamity which repeatedly befell the Harpurs of Swarkeston and Breadsall in the seventeenth century. Very few indeed were the families which maintained an unbroken male descent for more than a century or two. In Derbyshire the record is held by the Curzons of Kedleston, whose continuous tenure of that estate has lasted from the twelfth century to the present day. But the accidents of inheritance have carried Melbourne Hall to three different families since the last of the Cokes died childless in 1750, and hyphenated names such as Drury-Lowe (of Locko) or Wilmot-Horton (of Osmaston) show how often one family has taken over another by marrying its heiress. In these circumstances the Harpurs of Calke were fortunate in keeping up the succession of father and son without a break for a full three centuries, from 1622 to 1924. But in 1681 the continuity of the line depended on the survival of a child only a few months old, and in 1921 the premature death of the heir meant the end of the baronetcy and the succession of a female.

In practice, of course, however strict the settlements, no estate remained quite unchanged for two or three centuries on end. Each marriage was an opportunity to reappraise the situation, to make some part of the property subject to the settlement and to exclude some other part. Land might be bought or inherited and

very occasionally it might be sold, either to pay debts or to make a more advantageous purchase elsewhere. But the nucleus generally remained intact.

Overgrown remains of the lime-kilns which were once part of an important industry at the northern end of the park.

The nucleus of the Harpur estate consisted of the lands in the Trent valley south of Derby acquired by Richard Harpur through his marriage with the Findern heiress, lands at Findern, Potlock, Willington, Twyford, Stanton-by-Bridge, Repton, Ticknall and Swarkeston (above, p. 24). In addition the judge purchased property not only in other neighbouring villages such as Chellaston and Milton, but further afield in northern Derbyshire, in Staffordshire, Cheshire and Yorkshire. At a time when land was the only regular form of investment, these distant acquisitions were not necessarily intended to be retained indefinitely: some of them were simply a safe, income-yielding means of holding wealth until opportunities arose to purchase more land in the Trent valley. So in the course of time most of them were sold off with the exception of the Cheshire estate at Christleton (a bequest from Sir John Port), which was not disposed of until 1770. The Staffordshire purchase at Alstonfield was, however, to be the nucleus of a secondary Harpur estate which eventually covered some 20,000 acres in the moorlands round Longnor. At the very end of his life Judge Harpur made another important purchase. This was the manor of Hemington just over the Leicestershire border, which he bought from Walter Devereux, Earl of Essex, for £1300. In 1640 his grandson Sir John Harpur of Swarkeston acquired lands in Arleston and Sinfin from Sir Henry Blount, and in 1660 Sir John purchased the manor of Smisby from the family of Kendall who had owned it since the early sixteenth century.

Few of these acquisitions comprised an entire village. Even if they included manorial rights, there was often a second

Repton Park, a subsidiary house on the Harpur estate, remodelled by Sir Henry Crewe in the Gothic style in 1813 and pulled down by Sir Vauncey Harpur Crewe in a fit of rage in the 1890s.

manor in the same parish owned by someone else. But as opportunity offered, further properties, large and small, were bought in with the surplus income of what by the end of the sixteenth century was already one of the largest estates in Derbyshire. Sir John Harpur (d.1622) for instance, was active in filling in gaps in his property. In Alstonfield he enlarged his estate by purchase from the Catholic Fitzherberts, crippled by penal fines for their 'recusancy', and in 1599 he was able to acquire the rectorial estates of Alstonfield and Barrow-on-Trent from the Crown for £1789. His accounts show that between 1608 and his death in 1622 he spent over £7000 on miscellaneous purchases of property in Swarkeston, Ticknall, Willington, Hemington, Newton Solney and elsewhere. In Ticknall and around Calke the process of buying in odd tenements and parcels of land was to go on all through the eighteenth and nineteenth centuries well into the twentieth. At Ticknall the manorial rights were originally shared by three different lords, but by the end of the eighteenth century the Harpurs were effectively the sole lords of a single manor.

Calke itself was all Harpur property from its acquisition in 1622 onwards (above, p. 20), but much of the land round it was still in other ownership. As Lady Jane Coke put it in 1751, 'nothing embellishes a view more than seeing one's own land', and the Harpurs lost no opportunity of acquiring land that would enlarge their home territory. Immediately to the north much of Derby Hills belonged to the Cokes of Melbourne, and it was not until 1920 that the whole of this area passed into Harpur ownership. To the south the hamlet of Southwood was divided between the Harpurs and the Burdetts of Foremark, while Southwood itself was part of the estate of the Hastings family of Ashby-de-la-Zouch. In 1821 Sir George Crewe secured the Burdetts' land in Southwood hamlet in exchange for a detached part of his Repton property, and in 1860 his son bought Tatshall Fee, another small estate south of Ticknall.

Finally in 1900 Sir Vauncey paid £38,000 for Southwood and Old Parks, selling land in Alvaston and Boulton to pay for it. In 1954 the break-up of the Ferrers estate at Staunton Harold provided the opportunity to acquire an additional 129 acres of land close to the southern end of Calke Park.

At its height, the Harpur estate totalled some 33,000 acres, of which 20,000 were in Staffordshire, 13,000 in Derbyshire and 877 in Leicestershire. A substantial part of the Staffordshire lands consisted of moorlands suitable only for rough grazing, and this was until well into the nineteenth century a socially and agriculturally backward area whose value was, however, enhanced by the presence there of lead, copper and other minerals. The Derbyshire lands varied considerably in quality, but those in the Trent Valley included some of the most productive in the county, with rich pasture bordering the river Trent. Calke itself is geologically quite distinct from the rest of the Derbyshire estate. The name means 'chalk' or 'limestone', and Calke, together with Breedon, forms an outlying fragment of the great limestone formations of northern Derbyshire. Lime was much in demand both for building and for agricultural purposes, and the quarries round Calke and Breedon were the principal source of it in south Derbyshire and northern Leicestershire. Fisheries in the Trent between Repton and Swarkeston were another considerable asset until they were largely destroyed by pollution in the present century.

In the Muniment Room at Calke there was, in 1981, a vast accumulation of rentals, surveys, maps, ledgers and other documents which recorded the management of the Harpur estate over a period of four hundred years. In this short book no attempt can be made to write the economic history of the estate, but it must have experienced some of the vicissitudes which have affected English agriculture in the past – notably a mild depression between 1730 and 1750, a steady growth in income through the latter part of the eighteenth century, another depression after 1815, and a still worse one in the 1880s. It was, however, grain-growing areas that were most seriously affected by these economic storms, and the fact that much of the Harpur estate was devoted to stock-rearing and dairy-farming would have done something to protect it against the worst effects of agricultural depression. Of course cattle-farming had its own catastrophes. In about 1750 the guardians of the young Sir Harry Harpur were obliged to remit the rents of many of his tenants because they had lost 'the greatest part of their stock of cattle, by the contagious distemper, which now rageth in these parts'. And in 1783 disease was so rife among the cattle at Calke that Sir Harry himself commissioned a well-known medical expert called Thomas Kirkland to write a report on the problem, which was published.

But despite such setbacks, rentals and other estimates of the income generated by the estate provided a series of figures which (however imperfect) reflects periods of prosperity more strongly than it does those of depression. In the 1680s, during the minority of Sir John Harpur, the average net income accounted for by his guardians averaged just under £2000 p.a., but in 1692–3 it was

Overleaf: The Drawing Room.

over £3000. In 1709 a valuation of Sir John's estates gives the following figures:

Derbyshire and Hemington	£3282
Staffordshire	£2008
Cheshire	£85
	£5375
less annual payments	£880
	£4495

In 1732 the gross rental came to £6181, of which Derbyshire accounted for £4341, Staffordshire for £1640, and Cheshire for £200. In 1759 the estate was said to be worth £7200 a year, in 1769 £9697, in 1779 £11,998. By the time of Sir George Crewe's death in 1844 the rental, together with lands in hand, had gone up to £23,563, and in the 1870s the gross annual value of the whole estate was stated to be £36,366 p.a.

How did the Harpurs' agents achieve this apparently continuous growth in income throughout the two centuries from 1680 to 1880? Largely by agricultural improvement, supplemented to some extent by the exploitation of mineral resources. Agricultural improvement meant more flexible rotations of crops, the selective breeding of livestock, better drainage, and the treatment of the land with lime, marl and other fertilisers. Enclosure of the open fields was often a pre-requisite of improved agriculture, and so was the granting of leases to farmers, who could not be expected to lay out money on capital improvements without the security of tenure provided by a written lease. On the Harpur estate (as on many others) these symptoms of improvement can be observed from the mid-eighteenth century onwards. By then some former open fields had already been enclosed by agreement long before. There are indications that this was the case both at Swarkeston and at Calke. But between 1756 and 1789 ten places in which Harpur ownership was predominant were enclosed, either by agreement or by private Act of Parliament: in 1756 Milton, in 1764–5 Ticknall, in 1766 Repton and Stanton-by-Bridge, in 1768 Willington, in 1771 Derby Hills, in 1780 Findern, in 1784 Longnor, in 1788 Barrow-on-Trent, and in 1789 Hemington. In 1771, moreover, an Act was obtained to allow Sir Henry Harpur to grant leases on his estate. This was a facility of which, however, less use would be made in the future, partly because rising prices during the Napoleonic Wars made leases less attractive to landlords, and partly because relations between the Harpurs and their tenants-at-will were so good that (as was reported in 1806) 'improvement on an extensive scale' was carried on by the latter 'with as much confidence' as if they enjoyed 21-year leases.

Enclosures were fairly expensive (in 1789 the enclosure of Hemington cost the estate at least £754), but the outlay was justified by a substantially increased income. Evidence of this is provided by a rental originally drawn up in 1769 in which, ten years later, the agent, Robert Greaves, has 'advanced' the Derbyshire rents by 27 per cent and the Staffordshire ones by 17 per cent. The policy of improvement was continued by later agents. William Smith, who acted as agent both to Sir Henry Crewe and to his son Sir George, was himself an able and enterprising farmer whose New Leicester sheep and shorthorn cows were highly reputed. In Leicestershire he succeeded the celebrated breeder Robert Bakewell in the tenancy of Dishley Grange Farm, and in Derbyshire he was tenant both of the Burdetts' principal farm at Foremark and of Swarkeston Lows Farm on the Harpur-Crewe estate. While his agricultural expertise can only have been of benefit to the estate, and his 'skill and integrity' were not in doubt, his dual position both as agent and as tenant was something which would have seemed undesirable to a later generation. His successor, Thomas Grime, appointed in 1841, was, indeed, a man of a new type, who was in touch with such model estates as that of the Duke of Bedford at Woburn, from which he obtained a trained woodman to take charge of the woodlands at Calke. He and his successor John Shaw of Derby, who managed the estate for Sir John and Sir Vauncey, were the first of the professional agents, who in the present century have presided over the Estate Office at Ticknall.

While agriculture was being profitably exploited, industry was also being fostered. Like other Midland landowners the Harpurs did not reject industrial activity on their property. On the contrary they welcomed it as an additional source of income. In this way they contributed to the Industrial Revolution, which could easily have been retarded had they and their fellow landowners refused to allow the exploitation of mineral resources and the construction of canals and railways to transport their products. On the Harpur estate the principal industrial minerals were lead, copper, coal and lime. Of these only lime was available in sufficient quantity to produce a substantial regular income. Although there is evidence that they were being worked from the late sixteenth century to the middle of the nineteenth, the lead and copper mines on the Staffordshire estate seem never to have been very profitable, and the last of them, the Dale Mine at Warslow, went bankrupt in 1875. At various times coal was mined at Breadsall, Ticknall and Pistern Hill near Smisby, but the Harpur estate never owned a major colliery producing coal of the quality found, for instance, on the Hastings estate near Ashby.

The quarrying and burning of lime was, however, a flourishing industry which served both agriculture and building. As early as 1537, when leasing Calke to John Prest, the prior and canons of Repton had reserved the right to burn lime there for their own use. There were two principal limepits, one at Ticknall close to the northern entrance to the park and the other at Dimsdale or Dimminsdale to the south-east. It was chiefly to facilitate the carriage of lime from Ticknall, Dimsdale and Breedon southwards to Leicestershire, Warwickshire and Oxfordshire that a new canal from Coventry to Ashby was constructed in 1794–8. From its junction with the Coventry Canal near Nuneaton it ran absolutely level to Ashby, a distance of 30 miles, but beyond Ashby several locks would have been needed, and as the Company lacked capital to construct them, a tramway was substituted for the last five miles from Ashby to Ticknall. This was planned by the civil engineer Benjamin Outram. It ran north through Southwood and then along the west side of Calke Park before going underground in a tunnel which took it invisibly across the drive to the limepits to the east of the Ticknall Lodge. By this means lime was carried south while coal from the Moira Colliery near Ashby was brought north to fire the lime-kilns and the adjoining brick and tile works. While the dark Ticknall lime had an extensive market in the area served by the canal, the bricks and tiles appear to have been used mainly on the estate. The limeworks had ceased to function on a commercial scale by the end of the nineteenth century, but both they and the brick-yard continued in sporadic operation for estate purposes until 1941. The tramway was eventually acquired by the estate in 1913 and subsequently dismantled.

The contribution made to the family's income by mining, limeburning and brickmaking remains to be quantified, but to the visitor today the overgrown limepits, the abandoned kilns and the grassed-over track of the tramway are a reminder that industry once played its part in maintaining the position of the Harpur Crewes as the second wealthiest landowners in Derbyshire.

By the end of the nineteenth century the Harpur Crewe estate had reverted to a purely agricultural role. In an area where industrial activity was all around, Calke and its satellite farms became a rural oasis whose sanctity was jealousy guarded by Sir Vauncey. In 1887 he played a leading part in opposing a Bill to deepen and widen the Trent for steam navigation between Burton-on-Trent and Wilden Ferry near Shardlow. It would, he said, 'turn the river into a vast highway utterly destroying the fishing and wildlife shooting', while 'the steamers would stir up all the mud' and bring 'boatloads of excursionists' who would 'land when and where they chose to penetrate to Foremark and Ticknall ... a nice lot they would be too, out of all the large towns of Nottingham, Derby, Burton, Stoke and Newark'. His attitude was shared by neighbouring landowners, who combined to defeat the Upper Trent Navigation Bill in the House of Lords, but Sir Vauncey's obsession with birds threatened to turn his estate into a vast game-reserve at the expense of good husbandry. Not only were motor-cars banned in Calke Park because they might disturb the wildfowl, but his farm tenants were forbidden to cut and lay their hedges so as to provide the maximum cover for nesting birds. In 1900 he sold land on the outskirts of Derby that before long would have been ripe for housing development in order to purchase relatively unremunerative woods to the south of Calke. Post-war depression and a falling rent-roll led to further sales at Swarkeston, Stenson, Sinfin and Repton in 1919–23, and in November 1921 the financial situation was so threatening that Sir Vauncey panicked, and summarily dismissed nearly all the estate and domestic staff, who were out of work for six weeks before most of them were re-engaged.

In 1924 Mrs. Mosley inherited a badly neglected estate burdened with substantial Death Duties. The money was raised partly by selling more land south of Derby and also some of the

Breadsall estate. Mrs. Mosley's death in 1949 was followed by the sale of nearly 10,000 acres of the Staffordshire estate to pay Death Duties, but in 1971 a further sale of building land made it possible not only to buy back the land at Breadsall sold in the 1920s, but also to acquire the Breadsall Priory estate (which Sir John Harpur's guardians had vainly sought to purchase as far back as the 1690s).

In the 1970s the estate still consisted of 12,300 acres of agricultural land in Derbyshire and Staffordshire and 2000 acres of moorland in the latter county, but the sales necessitated by the Capital Transfer Tax due on the death of Charles Harpur-Crewe in 1981 have reduced it to less than 4000 acres. In Staffordshire 4695 acres of outstanding scenic value have been acquired by the government for the Peak Park, while the heart of the estate at Calke and Ticknall has passed to The National Trust together with the house and park.

The future Sir Vauncey and his bride are feted at Melbourne after their marriage in 1876.

6 THE HOUSE AND ITS CONTENTS

The House

FROM WHATEVER direction one approaches Calke Abbey, the house is hidden from view until the last moment. Its low-lying position in a hollow is a reminder of its monastic origin, for members of the religious orders liked secluded sites for their buildings. If Sir John Harpur had celebrated his coming of age by building a completely new mansion he would doubtless have placed it on higher ground, but what he did was to remodel the existing house, and behind the eighteenth-century walls there are substantial remains of an earlier house of sixteenth and early seventeenth-century date. Indeed the plan shows irregularities which may well be medieval in origin, though any remains of the priory which are still embedded in its walls have yet to be brought to light. We know that Richard Wendsley (who owned Calke from about 1575 to 1585) did much building there, and Henry Harpur may well have done more after he purchased the estate in 1622. By 1662, when Calke was assessed for the Hearth Tax, the house contained 23 hearths, which made it one of the most substantial houses in the county, though not quite so large as Swarkeston (28 hearths) and far smaller than Hardwick (114), Chatsworth (79) or Bretby (68). Inventories of the contents drawn up in 1670 and 1681 are not particularly informative, though both list the Hall, Dining Room, 'Yellow Parlour', Gallery and Kitchen and the earlier one also mentions a Drawing Room, a 'Silver Stuffe Chamber' and a Gate-house Chamber, among others.

If one penetrates into the central courtyard one can still see some architectural features that would have been visible when these inventories were made. On either side there are the battered remains of an arcaded loggia, two of whose arches retain diamond-ornamented keystones of Jacobean date, and in the walls there are vertical joints in the masonry which suggest an earlier date for the two corner projections against which the loggia abuts on either side. To the discerning eye other indications of adaptation and change will be apparent in the form of windows blocked up or reduced in size, though precisely why or when remains to be determined.

In the west front irregularities in the spacing of the windows and other details suggest that here, too, earlier masonry is hidden below the surface, and the existence of a blocked-up arch is recollected by those who saw the rendering removed in the 1960s. Further evidence of a complex architectural history is afforded by the strange recess at the junction of this wall and the kitchen pavilion, clumsily disguised by an overhanging cornice. Inside the house, two Elizabethan or Jacobean chimney-pieces survive (see p. 33), but the larger and finer one at least is said by family tradition to have been brought from Swarkeston, though if so the coat of arms with the baronet's symbol of a red hand must have been a later addition.

Whatever may be deduced from these and other clues, the form of the original house has been effectively disguised by its rebuilding in 1702–4. Sir John's new house was built of a grey sandstone from a quarry on his own land at Pistern Hill in nearby Smisby, supplemented by some similar stone purchased from another quarry at Donington. In the eighteenth century there were no general building contractors such as there are today, and masons, carpenters, bricklayers and other building craftsmen had normally to be separately employed. Many buildings were erected by a combination of direct labour for the main structure and piece or task-work for specialised details. This was the method adopted at Calke, where much of the work was done by men paid by the day.

Simplified plan of the ground floor in 1840, before the present Entrance Hall was made. The walls shown hatched are believed to be earlier than 1700.

AA corner projections, probably sixteenth century.
BB remains of early seventeenth-century loggia.
C former entrance to courtyard
D Back Stairs.
E Best Stairs.
F Corridor.
G Strong Room.
H Caricature Room.
J Base of Portico.

The Best Stairs, showing the original twin doors to the Saloon.

In the accounts the payments for building are mixed up with those for other purposes in a way which makes an exact calculation of the total cost impossible, but it was probably not less than £9000. Between the spring of 1702 and the summer of 1704 some 60 masons were employed for varying periods, while two of them named John Jordan and Simon Holt carried out various pieces of unspecified task-work. The principal carpenters and joiners appear to have been a Mr. Whelpdale and a Mr. Leech. The carver was a Mr. Wright, the painter Mr. Reading from Derby, and the plasterer Petty Dewick from Ashby-de-la-Zouch. The plumber, who was presumably responsible for one of the most attractive features of the house, its elaborately decorated downpipes and rainwater-heads (see p. 105), was George Braseby.

No architect is named, but in 1701 there were two payments to a 'surveyor' from Nottingham called Mr. Johnson. 'Surveyor' was a contemporary term for an architect, and this must have been the William Johnson of Nottingham who was employed by the canons of Southwell in that capacity in 1690, and by the borough of Nottingham 'to survey part of the free school in order to rebuild it' in 1708. A later payment to Mr. Whelpdale 'for surveying' seems to have been for measuring the workmanship of his fellow joiner Leech. A 'Mr. Huitt Surveyor' who received £5 in January 1705 may have been Thomas Hewitt of Shireoaks near Mansfield, a gentleman architect and landscape-gardener who was later to be Surveyor of the Royal Works, but is more likely to have been a French Protestant called 'Mr. Huett' who was much involved in the supervision of both building and gardening works at Chatsworth from 1694 to 1705. In either case this single payment just as the new house at Calke was nearly finished could relate to gardening rather than to architecture. William Johnson, on the other hand, was presumably involved in the preparations for rebuilding the house, but without further evidence it would be unwise to conclude that he designed it.

With its grand cornice supported by fluted pilasters* and its highly ornamented leadwork, the new house made a fine show. On closer inspection, however, some awkward features become apparent. Some of these have already been mentioned, and they arose from the adaptation and enlargement of an older building. Inside, the obliquity of the old wall which ran through the whole house from north to south resulted in one end of the great hall (or Saloon as it was later to be called) being markedly askew. More seriously, the centre of the new south façade did not correspond to the centre of the old internal courtyard (see p. 99). As it was the old courtyard which determined the siting of the twin staircases and the great hall to which they led, the Hall was, so to speak, out of step with the façade, with the result that its principal doorway is not centrally placed in the middle of its outer wall, and the sections of wall between its windows vary in width in a manner which makes better sense from outside than it does from within. These architectural irregularities suggest a certain lack of careful preliminary

* A pilaster is a shallow rectangular column set against a wall.

Detail of the Composite Order found on the corner pavilions. There is no precedent for this capital in English Baroque architecture and it appears to derive from the plate in Philibert de l'Orme's treatise on architecture (right).

thought, an impression which is borne out by a contemporary wise-crack that 'like Caulk House, the thing is done but nobody did it'.

Nevertheless, the result was a very large and handsome house, which in 1704 would have vied with Bretby (the neighbouring seat of the Stanhopes) for the distinction of being Chatsworth's only serious rival in south Derbyshire. Like Chatsworth, it consisted of three storeys, first a high basement, then two main floors, of which the upper was almost equal to the one below, and contained the principal bedrooms. This, at low-lying Calke, had the advantage of giving their occupants better views into the park than the rooms below. As the roof was flat there were no attics and the servants' quarters were behind the state rooms on the first floor.

In plan, the house is a rectangular block with projecting corner pavilions. These corner pavilions were a feature of country-house planning derived from France and found elsewhere in England at, for instance, Ragley Hall in Warwickshire (1679) and Hanbury Hall in Worcestershire (1701). Each pavilion was designed to contain, on at least one of its floors, an 'apartment' or set of rooms consisting of a bedroom, a private closet or study and a room for a personal servant. There might also be a 'withdrawing room' or sitting-room. In this way the occupant was provided with something like a self-contained flat (though without, of course, the modern amenities of running water and sanitation). At Calke such apartments still exist on the top and ground floors (see pp. 114–115).

Externally the pavilions were defined by fluted pilasters supporting a magnificently bold and elaborately decorated cornice (opposite). These pilasters are one of Calke's distinctive architectural features, for their capitals appear to be unique in English architecture. By the time Calke was built classical columns and pilasters had long been standardised into five 'orders', Tuscan, Doric, Ionic, Corinthian and Composite, each with its own capital. The Composite order combines elements from the Ionic and the Corinthian, and the capitals at Calke are an unusual form of the Composite seen among the ruins at Rome by a sixteenth-century French architect called Philibert de l'Orme and illustrated by him in a book of which the latest edition was published in Rouen in 1648 (opposite). How this little-known order came to be chosen for Sir John Harpur's new house must remain a matter for speculation, but if the Frenchman Huett from Chatsworth was indeed consulted then he could conceivably have suggested it.

Another distinctive feature of the house was the arrangement of twin staircases on either side of what appears originally to have been an entry leading into the courtyard. The southern end of this entry is now blocked off by a brick wall, but the archway at its northern end can still be seen from the courtyard. It was, of course, quite normal to have two staircases, one for the family and the other for the servants, but less so for them to rise side by side to either end of the Hall, whose north wall at Calke was originally pierced by four arched doorways – two at the top of each staircase.

Painting of the south front of the house showing the stone stairs designed by James Gibbs and built in 1728–9. The arms on the side of the coach are those of Sir Henry Harpur who succeeded in 1741 and died in 1748.

View of the house from the east before 1800. Note the stone stairs on the left where the portico now is and the secondary stairs up to a former doorway in the middle of the east front.

The eastern staircase was the 'Best Staircase', the western one the 'Back Stairs', but they appear to have been of identical plan and dimensions, the former (still existing) being distinguished from the latter (rebuilt on a different plan in 1841–2) by its superior joinery. The two staircases were linked at the bottom by a transverse corridor, now divided up, but still recognisable on the plan showing the ground floor as it was in about 1840 (see p. 99). From this plan it can be seen how the conflict between the external and internal axes of the house meant that the entrance at ground floor level could not be centrally placed in relation to the twin staircases. This must, nevertheless, have been the principal entrance to the house until 1728–9, when an external flight of stone stairs was built up to the hall doorway. These stairs, removed in 1806, are shown in a painting, dating from the 1740s, now in the Paul Mellon Collection at Yale (see p. 103). They were designed by the London architect James Gibbs, who had then just rebuilt the church of All Saints at Derby (to which Sir John Harpur subscribed ten guineas), and were constructed by Francis Smith of Warwick, the master mason employed at All Saints.

A flat-roofed house like Calke usually had a parapet above the cornice with ornamental urns at intervals, but no such parapet is visible either in the Mellon picture or in a later view of the east front of the house made before the existing balustraded parapet was constructed in the early nineteenth century (above). The accounts show that work on a parapet was indeed begun in 1709, but was subsequently abandoned for some unexplained reason.

In 1712–16 new stables completed Sir John Harpur's building programme. They form a substantial quadrangle, standing on rising ground to the north-west of the house, and partly concealed from it by trees. They were built by William Gilks, a local master-builder from Burton-on-Trent, almost certainly to his own designs, and cost some £1250. Unlike the house, they are built of a mellow red brick with stone dressings, but, like the house, they are embellished with highly decorative lead rainwater-heads and downpipes (below). The windows retain their original wooden mullions and transoms and many of the upper rooms still have floors not of wood but of a hard plaster made from lime-ash. Above the entrance archway is a domed lantern surmounted by an iron weathervane (see p. 108). The latter, together with the ornamental ironwork that supports it, was renewed in 1750 by the celebrated Derby smith, Robert Bakewell.

After 1729 the fabric of the house underwent no significant alteration for over 60 years. An important addition was however made to the stable-block in the form of a riding-school.

Decorative lead rainwater-heads on the stables. The boar is the Harpur family crest.

Its construction does not appear to be recorded in any of the surviving accounts, and as these are preserved in a continuous series throughout the eighteenth century except for the years from 1752 to 1772, it is likely that the riding school was built by Sir Harry Harpur some time between his coming of age in 1760 and the beginning of his first surviving account-book in 1772. It is a large plain brick building with a simple viewing gallery at one end. The roof is supported by immense wooden trusses of a kind illustrated in Francis Price's *British Carpenter*, the leading manual of Georgian structural carpentry.

To Sir Harry in the reign of George III the mansion built by his grandfather must have seemed architecturally outmoded, and it was doubtless for him that an unidentified architect made a set of designs for a completely new house in a style which suggests the influence (though not the hand) of Sir Robert Taylor (above). It must also have been in Sir Harry's time that a Staffordshire architect called Thomas Gardner made an unexecuted design for adding an attic storey to the house in order to provide more bedrooms (opposite). But it was left to his son to give to the great baroque house, with its grand but slightly gauche elevations, some of the sophisticated elegance of the later Georgian period. The architect chosen by the 'isolated baronet' to accomplish this transformation was William Wilkins the elder (d. 1815). He was the father of William Wilkins the younger (d. 1839), who was later to design the National Gallery and other well-known buildings. But although in retrospect overshadowed by his more celebrated son, the elder Wilkins was a highly competent architect whose career was furthered by the recommendations of his friend Humphry Repton, the fashionable landscape-gardener. In the 1790s he was best known as the designer of the Gothic Donington Hall for Sir Henry's neighbour Lord Moira, and it was as 'Lord Moira's architect' that in September 1793 the headmaster of Repton School met him when he dined with Sir Henry's agent, R. C. Greaves, at Ingleby.

Design for a new house at Calke, made by an unknown architect, probably in the 1760s.

Design by the Staffordshire architect Thomas Gardner for adding an attic storey, made probably about 1780.

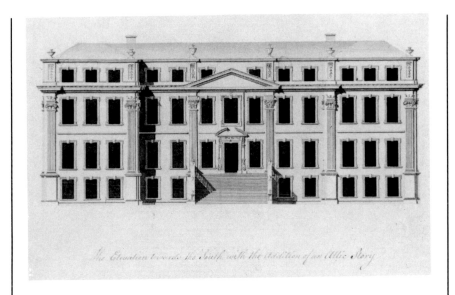

At Calke Wilkins' employment extended from 1793 to 1810 or 1811 and, although his curious design for a semi-circular portico (below) was made in 1794, it was not until 1806–8 that the existing portico was built. Its design presented a difficulty, for the projecting basement and stairs threatened to darken the front rooms on the ground floor, some of which Sir Henry used himself. The scheme for a semi-circular portico, with stairs inside the plinth, presumably represented an attempt to overcome this problem. The light iron stairs that Wilkins eventually provided at each side of the portico took away as little light as possible, but they must always have looked rather flimsy (see p. 110), and their disappearance in the present century need cause no regrets. The capitals of the four columns were copied from those of one of the temples on the Acropolis at Athens, known as the Erechtheum. The choice of a Greek version of the Ionic order showed that Sir Henry was abreast

Design by William Wilkins for a semi-circular portico, made in 1794.

The weather-vane on the stables, made by Robert Bakewell of Derby in 1750.

of contemporary architectural taste, and a full-scale model of one quarter of a capital was made for his inspection before he authorised its execution.

Inside the house Wilkins' main task was to create a new dining room on the first floor in the south-west pavilion. The location of the original dining room is not certain, and a 'New Dining Roome' is mentioned in 1729, when Thomas Eborall, a joiner from Warwick, was paid £153 for wainscoting it and for other associated works. At all events it was in 1793–4 that the present Dining Room received its elegant neo-classical interior, with Ionic recess for the sideboard and walls decorated with paintings in an antique Roman style. Unfortunately the relevant bills have not come to light, but in 1794 'the man that polished the Pillars in the dining room' was given 10s. 6d. 'by Sir Henry's orders', and in 1795 a visitor to Calke inspected 'two new rooms which had just been finished at an immense expense'. She found the Dining Room 'too gaudy to please me', but 'the withdrawing room' she considered 'more plain and elegant'. The Drawing Room in the southeast pavilion (see pp. 92–93) is basically a room of 1793–4, but in 1809 or 1810 it was further embellished to their own designs by the fashionable cabinet-makers Tatham and Bailey. To them are due the two gilded mirrors and much of the furniture. 'I hope', Thomas Tatham was later to write, 'Sir Henry likes the drawing room and have no doubt that it is really a handsome apartment – at least I have done my best to make it so.'

The third room designed by Wilkins for Sir Henry was the Library, which occupies the southern half of the east front (see p. 10). It was formed out of two smaller rooms and lined with bookshelves which are canted at both ends to give spatial interest. Above each section of shelving there hangs a rolled map, one of Europe, one of England and Wales, and others of the various Midland counties. These, like the writing table, with 'black à la grec border', library steps and chairs, were supplied by Tatham and Bailey. The Library was completed in 1805, when the walls were painted green. Outside, Wilkins built a long balcony to provide a promenade from which particularly attractive views of the park are obtained (see p. 121).

While the Library was being created inside the house, Wilkins was building three new gate-lodges. They were, as he himself put it, 'simple in the design, yet sufficiently marking an Approach to a House of some consequence'. Those at the Ticknall and Heath End entrances to the park each consisted of two simple archways for pedestrians on either side of an iron gate with a detached porter's lodge close by, but at the Middle Lodge Wilkins showed his mettle as a serious neo-classical architect. For in its clear-cut arch springing only a few feet from the ground we can probably detect a reminiscence of an archway designed by the celebrated French architect Ledoux in front of a Parisian mansion, the Hotel Thélusson. This in its turn recalled a half-buried arch in Rome well known from engravings by Piranesi and others. Wilkins had previously made an identical design for a lodge at Ossington Hall in Nottinghamshire that had not been adopted, and he was doubtless gratified to see it built at Calke instead (see p. 51).

When Sir George Crewe succeeded his father in 1819 his first architectural enterprise was, predictably, to rebuild the church in the park, and it was not until 1841 that he turned his attention to the house. A thorough overhaul ensued, under the direction of Henry Isaac Stevens, an architect from Derby best known for a number of unremarkable Gothic churches, among them the one at Ticknall. Stevens was anxious to improve the internal circulation by building a three-storey corridor across the southern side of the central courtyard, but this did not find favour with his employer.

The front of the house photographed in 1886, soon after the death of Sir John Harpur Crewe. In accordance with custom a 'hatchment' representing the arms of the deceased baronet has been placed over the main entrance. The iron stairs (since removed) can be seen on either side of the portico.

However, on the ground floor a new Entrance Hall was made by throwing two existing rooms into one, and the left-hand of the two staircases was rebuilt in stone and cut off from the Hall, the better to serve its function as a back stair. Upstairs a fractured beam over the Library necessitated the complete renewal of the ceiling to Stevens's designs, and the bookshelves were heightened to accommodate the social, religious and political literature that Sir George was acquiring.

The most important of Stevens's works was, however, the remodelling of the Saloon. Before 1841 this grand room, the ceremonial centre of the house, was askew at the east end because of the retention here of the ancient wall already mentioned. Stevens straightened out this end of the room, providing a new chimney-piece, but merely readjusting the pilasters and broken pediment that frame it. Above the level of the cornice he divided the wall up into panels for the hanging of family portraits, and he remodelled the ceiling completely with recessed compartments displaying the Harpur family crest (a boar) between finely moulded bands of

ornament. The whole was achieved with considerable dexterity, and suggests that Stevens had abilities as a classical architect for which his predominantly ecclesiastical practice afforded too little scope.

Since 1841–2 there have been no significant alterations to the fabric of Calke Abbey. In 1865–6 Henry Marley Burton carried out a number of minor repairs and improvements, but his proposals for corridors round the courtyard and other major alterations found no more favour with Sir John Harpur Crewe than they had done with his father, and apart from the introduction of the telephone in 1928 and of electricity in 1962, no subsequent owner of Calke has even contemplated modernising the house. Now it is undergoing its first major repair since 1842, under the direction of Mr. Rodney Melville of the John Osborne Partnership in Leamington.

The Contents

Calke Abbey is a house where for the last 150 years, scarcely anything has been thrown away. Before that, furniture, pictures and personal possessions were lost, destroyed or given away as they have always been by succeeding generations looking with a careless or a critical eye on their parents' possessions. Successive inventories of 1670, 1681, 1741, 1748 and 1821 are full of objects that cannot be traced today. Indeed, of those listed in 1670 only one – a 'liverie cubbord' – can tentatively be identified with a piece of furniture of that description now in a room on the ground floor. A considerable amount of Georgian furniture remains, including some handsome gilded wall-mirrors and a chamber organ in an elaborately carved mahogany case, but no single room is furnished as it was in the time of the first three Georgian Baronets. Pictures, too, have come and gone, and so have china and silver. But at Calke the normal process of removal and renewal was arrested about the middle of the nineteenth century. Sir George had fortunately retained most of the elegant furniture made for his father by Tatham and Bailey. He acquired some more – including a large wardrobe by Gillow of Lancaster now in the Pink Room – when he overhauled the house in the 1840s, and in the 1850s Georgiana Lady Crewe interspersed the existing Tatham and Bailey furniture in the Drawing Room with her own embroidered chairs and occasional tables to create that opulently overcrowded atmosphere so characteristic of the period (see p. 9). Since then, apart from the remorseless advance of Sir Vauncey's stuffed birds, the only significant changes have been the acquisition of certain pieces of furniture carved by the Egyptologist Sir Gardner Wilkinson (see p. 85), the bequest in 1930 by Sir George's daughter Mary of the Flemish cabinet now in the Dining Room, and the importation, in the 1920s, of Godfrey Mosley's furniture from Willington Grange, including some formerly at Burnaston House. Much of this found its way into the Caricature Room and the adjoining room still known as 'Colonel Mosley's Study'.

Calke today is therefore a treasury of Victorian life and Victorian taste with a substratum of Georgian furniture, pictures, silver and china. In general the Georgian survivals are of greater

The Saloon, with family portraits round the walls and Tilly Kettle's fine painting of Lady Frances Harpur and her son in the manner of Reynolds over the fireplace.

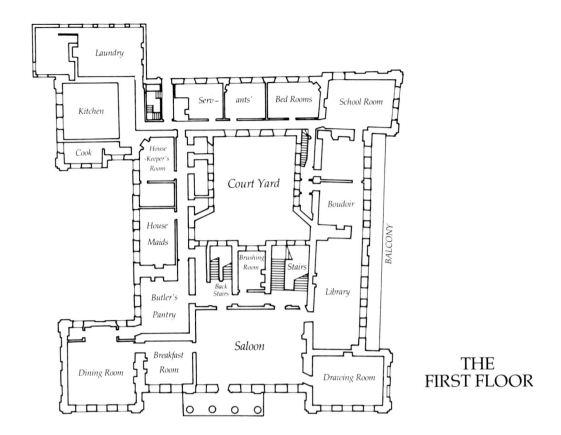

Laundry

Kitchen

Cook

House-Keeper's Room

House Maids

Butler's Pantry

Serv- ants' Bed Rooms

School Room

Court Yard

Boudoir

BALCONY

Brushing Room

Back Stairs

Stairs

Library

Saloon

Dining Room

Breakfast Room

Drawing Room

THE
FIRST FLOOR

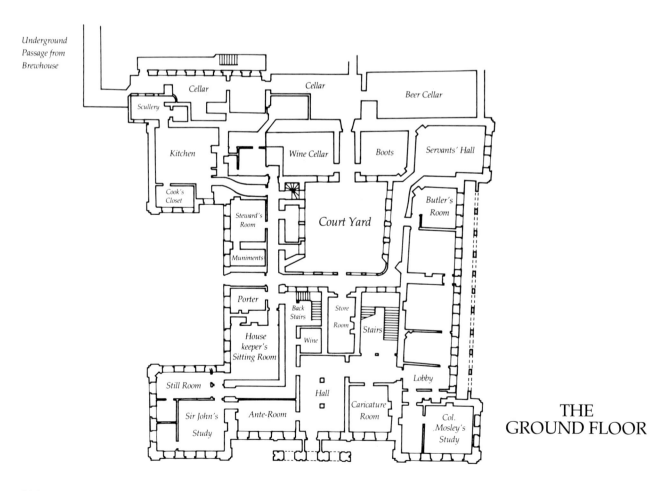

Underground Passage from Brewhouse

Cellar

Cellar

Beer Cellar

Scullery

Kitchen

Wine Cellar

Boots

Servants' Hall

Cook's Closet

Steward's Room

Court Yard

Butler's Room

Muniments

Porter

Back Stairs

Store Room

Stairs

House keeper's Sitting Room

Wine

Still Room

Lobby

Sir John's Study

Ante-Room

Hall

Caricature Room

Col. Mosley's Study

THE
GROUND FLOOR

114

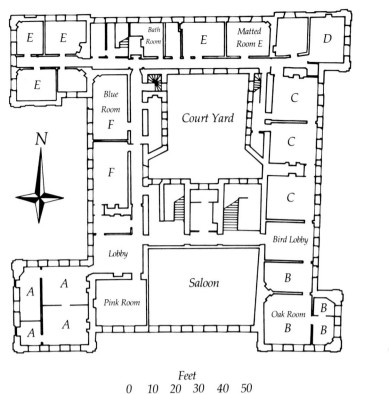

THE TOP FLOOR

Feet
0 10 20 30 40 50

Plan of the top floor. This floor contained the principal bedrooms, and all the owners of Calke have slept on this floor, with the exception of Sir George Crewe, whose bedroom was the room on the first floor later used as the School Room. A is the apartment occupied by Lady Frances Harpur after (and perhaps before) the death of her husband in 1789, and by Sir John and Lady Harpur Crewe from 1845 to 1886. B is the apartment occupied by Sir Henry and Lady Crewe 1792–1819. C are the rooms occupied by Sir Henry and Lady Caroline Harpur 1741–8. D is Sir Vauncey Harpur Crewe's bachelor room. E are rooms occupied by children, governesses, etc. F are the rooms occupied by Sir Vauncey and Lady Harpur Crewe 1886–1924.

intrinsic merit than the objects of later date. Certainly there are no individual masterpieces of Victorian design, for none of the later owners of Calke was a discriminating patron of the arts who sought out designers of distinction. But if there is nothing exceptional or avant-garde at Calke, the authentic atmosphere of a Victorian household can be appreciated here as nowhere else. For Calke is a house where time has (visually speaking) stood still for well over a hundred years. As the photographs on pages 9–12 testify, the State Rooms remain almost precisely as they were in 1886, the year of Sir John Harpur Crewe's death. One can walk into them knowing that if one had done so at any time during the last hundred years they would have looked exactly the same, and that is an historical experience that is almost unique to Calke.

Elsewhere in the house the contents were in 1981 in much less good order. Upstairs, in bedroom after bedroom, the accumulated personal possessions of four or five generations of the family lay in greater or lesser disorder, for at Calke successive owners, instead of clearing out their predecessors' belongings, have tended simply to close the door and move to another room. Indeed, it is remarkable that scarcely a single owner of Calke has chosen to occupy the same bedroom as his immediate predecessor. Thus Sir John Harpur (d.1741) appears to have favoured the west side of the house, Sir Henry (d.1748) the east. The south-east pavilion was occupied by the 'isolated baronet', the south-west one by Sir John Harpur Crewe. Sir George and his lady slept in the room on the first floor in the north-east pavilion, while Sir Vauncey and Lady Isabel chose a room in the middle of the west front. However Sir Vauncey's bachelor room in the north-east pavilion remained (and still remains) exactly as it had been in his youth, full of hunting trophies,

Inside the courtyard: On the left are the remains of the seventeenth-century loggia.

trays of butterflies, cabinets of polished stones and a prodigious collection of walking-sticks of every shape and size (see p. 6).

Amid the muddle and confusion which at present prevails in so many of the rooms at Calke many interesting and evocative objects can be discerned. Some of these things were normal household goods in their day: they represent the archaeology of daily life. Such are the china, the linen, the kitchen and laundry equipment, the leather fire-buckets, the patent 'Harden Star Hand Grenade' fire extinguishers, the tools in the smithy and the joiner's shop. They illustrate the laborious and labour-intensive world of domestic service before the advent of plastics, electricity and central heating.

But upstairs the drawers and cupboards open to reveal the relics of a privileged life: tissue-lined cartons containing Victorian dolls in mint condition, toy soldiers from Germany, their red coats as brilliant as on the day they were bought, a boxful of wooden building blocks, which on being assembled is found to represent the International Exhibition Building of 1862, a case of presentation silver, books full of dried flowers, black-bordered writing paper still in mourning for Sir Vauncey's death in 1924, even the formal responses to the only invitations that Charles Harpur-Crewe ever issued to the Derbyshire gentry (it was when he was High Sheriff in 1961). Clothes and uniforms abound, from a bundle labelled 'Sir Harry's stockings' to an exquisite silk coat that belonged to Sir Henry Crewe. The blue uniform of the Calke Troop of the Derbyshire Yeomanry is there, complete with elegant metal badges displaying the Harpur arms, but of the livery worn by the household servants there survives only a boxful of brass buttons ornamented with the Harpur and Crewe crests. Musical instruments range from a harpsichord (found in the stables) made by the celebrated Burkat Shudi (the predecessor of the firm of Broadwood) in 1741, or a mandolin (discovered by the writer behind a bookcase) by Donato Filano dated 1761, to a Victorian barrel organ by Flight and Robson.

Then there are the things deliberately collected as opposed to those accidentally preserved. Chief among these are, of course, Sir Vauncey's stuffed birds, which make much of the house look like an old-fashioned natural history museum. But the glass-fronted cabinets and cases in the Saloon and elsewhere contain many other curiosities and antiquities: specimens of minerals collected by Sir John Harpur Crewe; examples of the dark brown pottery which was made in large quantities in Ticknall from the sixteenth century until about 1876; two Bronze Age swords found probably in the River Trent; and an ivory model of a Chinese pagoda given to Jane Lady Crewe by a friend in the East India Company's service.

All these things, and many others, will in due course be displayed by The National Trust. Some of the more notable of them are illustrated in this book.

7 THE PARK AND GARDENS

Opposite: Map of Calke Park, showing the chain of ponds before the easternmost one (F) was absorbed by the reservoir made in 1956–8.

Below: Map of Calke made in the middle of the eighteenth century, showing the formal gardens and avenues and the ponds before enlargement later in the century.

THE DRIVE TO Calke Abbey from the Ticknall Lodge is nearly two miles long. First there is a lime-avenue to traverse, then a second lodge, then a glimpse of picturesque ponds surrounded by stag-headed oaks. At last a sudden turn reveals the house in a hollow surrounded by parkland, with its satellite stable-block to one side, the church to the other, and the waters of the modern reservoir in the distance.

With the possible exception of the oaks, it is entirely a man-made landscape. For the park which surrounds Calke Abbey is just as much a human artefact as the house itself. If we could see

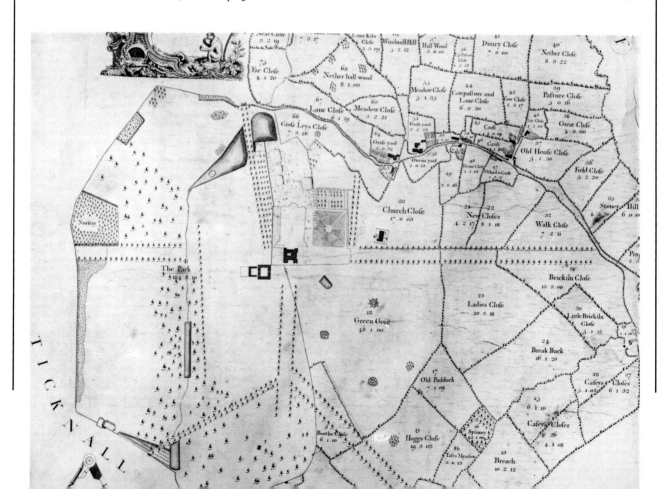

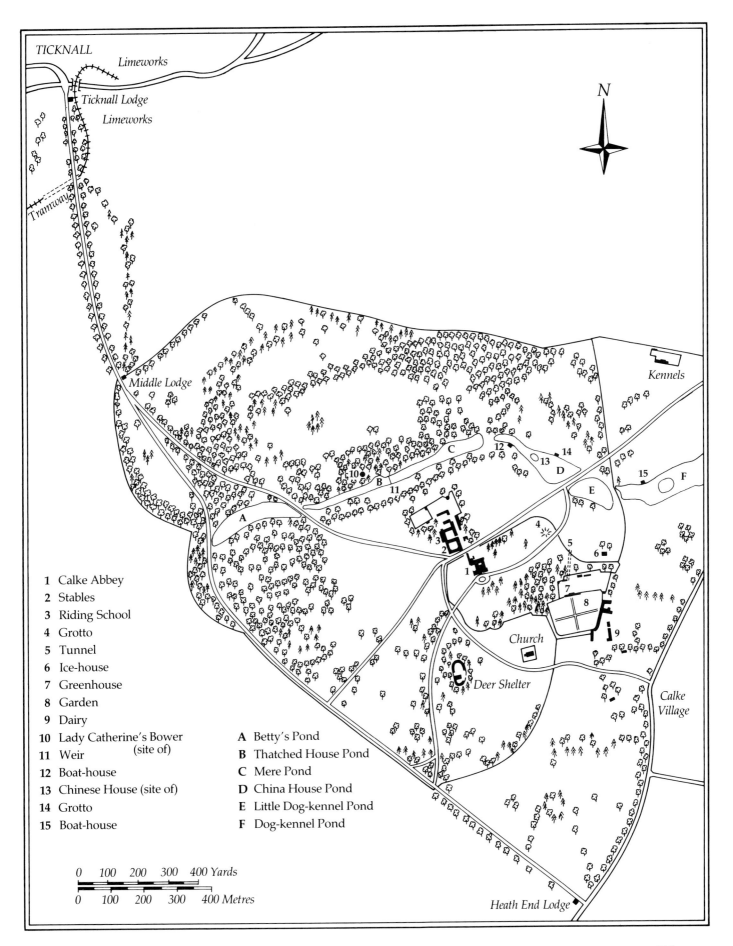

TICKNALL

Limeworks

Ticknall Lodge

Limeworks

Tramway

N

Middle Lodge

Kennels

C

12
13   14

10 B   D

11   E

15   F

A

4

3   5

2   6

1   7

8

9

1 Calke Abbey

2 Stables

3 Riding School

4 Grotto   *Church*

5 Tunnel

6 Ice-house

7 Greenhouse   *Deer Shelter*   *Calke Village*

8 Garden

9 Dairy

10 Lady Catherine's Bower
                    (site of)
11 Weir

12 Boat-house   **A** Betty's Pond

13 Chinese House (site of)   **B** Thatched House Pond

14 Grotto   **C** Mere Pond

15 Boat-house   **D** China House Pond

                         E Little Dog-kennel Pond

                         F Dog-kennel Pond

0   100 200 300 400 Yards

0   100 200 300 400 Metres

Heath End Lodge

Calke as it was in 1622 when Henry Harpur acquired the estate, we should hardly recognise the place. Where there is now parkland there would then have been enclosed fields, where there are now picturesque lakes there would have been at best small ponds, and near the church there would have been a village street containing a score of cottages. Round the house even the contours would have been different, for in the eighteenth century much smoothing and levelling of the ground took place.

If we look at a mid eighteenth-century map (the earliest that has survived, see p. 118) we can see that the park was still quite small (only 184 acres), and that the avenues of limes planted by Sir John Harpur soon after he rebuilt the house ran across several field boundaries and were not intended to define carriage-drives. Their function was purely visual, but as such their effectiveness must have been limited, as they were centred on a house from which, because of the terrain, scarcely any of them would have been fully visible. Only along the approach from Ticknall (off the map to the left) did an avenue and a drive coincide, and there the roadway is still lined with Sir John's limes (or their successors). As for the ponds, they

The lime avenue to Ticknall.

were neither tamed into canals nor enlarged to picturesque effect. Their beauties, such as they were, were augmented by a grotto, a gazebo and a 'Chinese House', to be described later.

So in terms of formal landscape, Calke can never have been a great success. But by the middle of the eighteenth century formality was going out of fashion and the aim of the garden designer was to create a landscape in which irregular sheets of water and informally grouped trees were combined to create views as carefully composed as if they formed part of a picture. With its steeply sloping valleys and its abundance of water, Calke had all the essential elements out of which to create an outstanding English landscape park. It was Sir Harry Harpur who first realised the picturesque potentialities of Calke. In 1776 the landscape-gardener William Eames, whose base was then near Derby and whose practice was rapidly developing in the Midland counties, was paid 14 guineas 'for Plans and Estimates for Gardens and pleasure Ground at Caulk'. Eames's plans seem, however, to have been limited to the vicinity of the house, and it was not until 1785 that the landscaping of the park was begun on a large scale. During the next four years some £3600 were spent on 'work at the nursery and Plantations and leveling the ground before the House'. The Hon. John Byng observed these works in progress when he visited Calke in June 1789, only a few months after Sir Harry's death. 'Many men', he noted, 'are employ'd in blowing up a long extent of hill, in front [of the house] which is done, at perhaps no expense, as they burn the limestone of which it consists.'

Young Sir Henry continued the process of improvement, which became a major preoccupation of his solitary life, and by the time of his death in 1819 had transformed the park into a landscape

The park as seen from the Library: a Victorian water-colour by Sir Gardner Wilkinson.

The grotto built in 1809–10. From a Victorian water-colour drawing by G. R. Vawser.

The Greenhouse or Conservatory built in 1778. A photograph taken in 1943.

of striking beauty. It was now enlarged to its present extent, and on the south its seclusion was ensured by demolishing several cottages in the dwindling village of Calke. The new limits were marked by gates and lodges designed by the architect Wilkins, one on the south and two on the north, at either end of the long drive to Ticknall. The limeburning and brickmaking at the latter village was largely screened by strategically-placed shelter-belts, and the waggons of lime on their way to Ashby went underground at the point where they had to cross the northern drive. The existing ponds were enlarged and linked to form a chain of lakes set between steeply rising banks clothed with ancient oaks, while elsewhere judiciously planted clumps of trees created a picturesque landscape enlivened by two herds of deer, one red, the other fallow. It was for their benefit that a double deer-shelter was erected to the south of the church.

In 1809–10 a new grotto, a cascade and a Gothic bridge were constructed under the direction of an architect called Samuel Browne. The grotto (see p. 121) remains in a dilapidated state to the east of the house, and the cascade is represented by the weir at one end of Mere Pond, but the bridge was lost when the Staunton Reservoir covered its site (east of Dog-kennel Pond) in 1956–8. By 1819 the landscape within the park was established in the form in which we see it today, though it was, of course, to be many years before the trees all grew to maturity. Outside the park to the south

The Georgian grotto on the north side of China House Pond.

and west some further shelter-belts were planted in the early nineteenth century, partly by Sir Henry and partly by Sir George. Many of the 23,000 sapling trees that the latter purchased from a Derby nursery in 1840–1 were probably destined to extend the plantations at Pokers Leys and Long Alders.

Within the park and in the immediate vicinity of the house there was in the early eighteenth century a walled garden. Its construction followed the building of the house in 1702–4. The best advice was taken. In 1702 the King's gardener George London was paid £2 3s. 'for his garden draughts', and in the same year 'Messrs. Geo. London & Hen. Wise' received £28 6s. 'as per bill of particulars', no doubt for plants from their well-known nursery at Brompton Park. In 1711 Mr. Wise's bill 'for Box & Yews etc.' came to £2 14s., and in 1713 Mr. London charged £14 for '5500 Hornbeame Setts that was sent to Caulk'. Then in 1721 Mr. Bridgeman, another celebrated master-gardener, was paid three guineas 'for a Draft for the alteration of the Ground before the house'. In the previous year new ornamental ironwork for the garden had been supplied by Robert Bakewell at a cost of £70. The mid-Georgian estate map (see p. 118) offers a little help in interpreting these payments. On the level ground immediately to the east of the house there is an enclosed area terminated by a triply curved wall or fence, which Bakewell's ironwork may well have adorned. To the south there is a square garden laid out with radiating segments. The focus of

The church as seen from the house.

interest would presumably have been a parterre inside the walled or fenced area. There was a fountain, for which 'white gravel' was bought in 1712, while 'red gravel' was bought 'for the new garden'.

This formal garden, together with Bakewell's ironwork, was swept away as part of the late eighteenth-century improvements, and in the late 1770s a new walled garden was created on the rising ground to the south-east of the house. The making of this garden followed the employment of William Eames to make 'Plans and Estimates' in 1776, and the layout may well have been his. It comprised a Flower Garden, a 'Physic Garden' and a Kitchen Garden and included the Greenhouse or Conservatory built in 1778 and at present in a ruinous condition. Surviving lists of plants show that in the time of Sir Henry (d.1819), apples, pears, plums, peaches and nectarines were growing against the garden walls. The Physic Garden contained many different varieties of carnations and several of auriculas. In the Stove (or hothouse) there were various exotic plants, including aloes, cacti, crassulas, mimosas, oleanders and passion flowers, while the Conservatory contained lime, lemon and orange trees, several myrtles and many geraniums (i.e. pelargoniums). By the 1820s there were 58 varieties of geraniums, including one named 'Calkensis' and another 'Crewensis'. These were ephemeral hybrids which never found their way into the botanical lists, but a small yellow wallflower named *Cheiranthus Harpur-Crewe* is still widely cultivated. It was raised not at Calke but in the Rectory garden at Drayton Beauchamp in Buckinghamshire, where between 1860 and his death in 1883 the Revd. Henry Harpur Crewe (son of Sir Henry Crewe's younger son the Revd. H. R. Crewe) was a well-known botanist and gardener.

Immediately to the east of the walled garden a new dairy was built in 1780. This was a working dairy rather than an ornamental one, and substantial quantities of cheese were made here for sale as well as for domestic consumption. The building still exists as part of the Home Farm, and the Hopton Stone dressers upon which the pans of milk were placed to allow the cream to rise remain in place, though no longer in use. Above them the walls were formerly lined with plain white tiles supplied by Wedgwood.

It remains to describe the ornamental buildings associated with the ponds in the early Georgian landscape. Of these only the grotto survives. It is built into the bank on the north side of China House Pond. Behind a symmetrical stone façade framing a rusticated arch there is a semicircular room overlooking the pond. The exact date of this structure is not known, but in 1746–7 Sir Henry and Lady Caroline Harpur built the 'Chinese House' which gave its name to the pond. It stood on a small island in the pond and was evidently an exotic summerhouse of a kind fashionable in the middle of the eighteenth century. It was ornamented with dragons drawn by a man from the studio of the decorative painter Lewis Goupy and was surmounted by an iron vane made by Robert Bakewell. Inside it there were eight chairs and a mahogany table. Its plan can just be discerned on the Georgian map of the estate (see p. 118). On the bank above Mere Pond there was another summerhouse or gazebo known as 'Lady Catherine's Bower'. A

125

The house (left) and church in the time of Sir John Harpur Crewe (d.1886), with Longhorn cattle and Portland sheep in the foreground.

flight of stone steps still leads up to its site, which is marked by a polygonal foundation about 15 feet in diameter. It was named after, and must presumably have been built for, Catherine Crewe, who married Sir John Harpur in 1702. The trunk of a dead beech-tree nearby bears several initials and dates cut by Georgian visitors, including 'I H 1747', perhaps for Catherine's younger son John.

Apart from the house itself and its offices, the only other building in the park is the church. This was built in 1826 at the expense of Sir George Crewe, and is a simple rectangular structure with a west tower, designed in the Gothic style by some local architect as yet unidentified. It is said to incorporate some of the walls of its predecessor, a humble building whose bell-cote a visitor in 1789 could mistake for a pigeon-house. The tracery of the windows is of cast-iron and was made in a Derby foundry. Inside there is a monument by Sir Henry Cheere to Sir John Harpur (d.1741) and his wife, another by Sir Edgar Boehm to Sir John Harpur Crewe (d.1886) and a third to Sir Vauncey (d.1924). Other members of the family are buried in the churchyard.

INDEX

Agriculture, 91, 93–5
Alexander, Arthur, 83
Alstonfield, Staffs., 24, 89, 90
Alvaston, Derbys., 91
Anne, Princess (d.1759), 46
Arleston, Derbys., 89
Ashby-de-la-Zouch, Leics., 30, 36, 68, 90, 95, 96, 101, 122
  Canal, 95
Augustinian Order, 13, 15

Badcock, see Lovell
Bainbridge, Robert, 20, 28
Bainbridge, Robert, jr., 20, 33
Bakewell, Robert, ironsmith, 41, 105, 108, 123, 125
Bakewell, Robert, stock-breeder, 95
Bancroft, Thomas, poet, 30
Barham House, Herts., 50, 57
Barrow-on-Trent, Derbys., 24, 90, 94
Bassett, Thomas, 31
Baxter, James, coachman, 66
Beaumont, Barbara, 31
Beaumont family, 20, 31, 33
Bedford, Duke of, 95
Bedford School, 75
Beer, consumption of, 13
Bentley, Sir John, 30
Birds, stuffed, see Ornithology
Blackwell, Alice, 17
Blackwell, Richard, 17
Blore, Staffs., 31
Blount, Sir Henry, 89
Bloxholme, Lincs., 43
Bloxam, Rev. R. R., 58
Boehm, Sir Edgar, sculptor, 73, 126
Boulton, Derbys., 91
Boulton & Fothergill, silversmiths, 45
Bradbourne, Frances, 17
Bradbourne, William, 17
Braseby, George, plumber, 101
Breadsall, Derbys., 36, 95
  Estate, 31, 97
  Priory, 13, 97
  Rector, 56, 64
Breedon-on-the-Hill, Leics.
  Priory, 13
  Quarries, 91, 95
Bretby Hall, Derbys., 98, 102
Bridgeman, Charles, landscape-gardener, 123
Browne, Samuel, architect, 52, 122
Buckingham, George Villiers, Duke of, 34
Burdett family, 90, 95
  Sir Robert, 72, 75
  Sir Thomas, 34
Burke, Sir Bernard, 68
Burnaston House, Derbys., 74, 111
Burton, Henry Marley, architect, 70, 111
Burton-on-Trent, Staffs., 24, 36, 78, 96, 105
Byng, Hon. John, 121
Byron, Sir John, 30

CALKE
  ABBEY
    Bedrooms, 7, 102, 115
    Bed, State, 46, 78
    Bird Lobby, 73
    Boudoir, 19
    Breakfast Room, 23, 63
    Caricature Room, 55, 111
    Cellars, 13, 60
    Chimney-piece, 33
    Courtyard, 98, 109, 111
    Dining Room, 52, 98, 108–9, 111
    Drawing Room, 9, 47, 52, 70, 78, 109, 111
    Entrance Hall, 61, 63, 85, 110
    Furniture, 37, 111–17
    Joiner's Shop, 78
    Kitchen, 58, 98
    Library, 11, 52–3, 109, 110
    Loggia, 98, 117

    Muniment Room, 78, 91
    Pink Room, 111
    Plans of. 99, 114–15
    Portico, 107
    Riding School, 106
    Saddle Room, 79
    Saloon, 12, 63, 70, 110, 117
    Smithy, 78
    Stables, 43, 78, 105, 108
    Stairs, 101, 103–4
  CHURCH, 34, 41, 42, 57, 73, 109, 120, 126
  CONSERVATORY, 122, 125
  DAIRY, 125
  GARDENS, 123, 125
  PARK, 51, 118–26
    map of, 119
    Bridge, Gothic, 122
    Cascade, 122
    Chinese House, 121, 125
    Deer-shelter, 122
    Grottoes, 121, 123
    Lady Catherine's Bower, 125
    Lodges, 51, 52, 96, 109, 118, 122
    Ponds, 120, 122, 125
  PECULIAR JURISDICTION, 16–17
  PLACE-NAME, 91
  PRIORY, 13–17, 98
  VILLAGE, 120, 122
Cambridge
  Corpus Christi College, 43
  Trinity College, 67
Capital Transfer Tax, 79, 82, 86, 97
Caroline, Queen, 46
Cattle, 68, 91, 95, 126
Cave, Rev. C. H., 76
Cecil, Sir Robert, 29
Cavendish, Lord George, 44
Cavendish, Lord James, 40
Cerveteri, Italy, Étruscan tomb, 85
Cheere, Sir Henry, sculptor, 41, 42, 126
Cheiranthus Harpur Crewe, wallflower, 125
Chellaston, Derbys., 24, 68, 89
Chester, races, 45: St. Werburgh's Abbey, 15
Chester, Hugh d'Avranches, 2nd Earl of, 15
Chester, Matilda, Countess of, 15–16
Chester, Ranulph, 5th Earl of, 15
Chester, Richard, 3rd Earl of, 15
Christleton, Cheshire, 89
Church Gresley Priory, Derbys., 13
Civil War, 32, 43
Clarke, Godfrey Bagnall, 45
Coke, Elizabeth, 40
Coke, Lady Jane, 90
Coke, Thomas, Vice-Chamberlain, 40
Coke family, 38, 88
Costumes, 117
Crewe, Catherine, see Harpur, Catherine, Lady
Crewe, Sir George, 8th Bart. (d.1844), 57–66, 90, 94, 95, 109–10, 111, 115, 123, 126
Crewe, Sir Henry, 7th Bart. (d.1819), 47, 48–57, 95, 106, 107, 109, 115, 117, 121, 123, 125
Crewe, Rev. Henry Robert, 50, 56, 57, 58, 64
Crewe, Isabel Jane, 66, 71
Crewe, Jan., Lady (née Whittaker), 58, 66, 117
Crewe, Mary Adeline, 66, 111
Crewe, Nathaniel, 3rd Lord, Bishop of Durham, 37, 47
Crewe, Nanny, Lady (née Hawkins), 49, 58
Crewe, Thomas, 2nd Lord, 37
Crewe of Steane, barony, 56
Crousaz, Louis de, 44, 48
Cruickshank, George, 55
Cumberland, Henry Frederick, Duke of, 40, 88
Cuyp, Albert, painter, 63

D'Agar, Charles, painter, 38
Dale Abbey, Derbys., 17
Darley Abbey, Derbys., 13
Davis, William, painter, 23

Death Duties, 75, 86, 96
Deer, 37, 122
Derby, 36, 67, 68, 78, 96, 105, 109, 121, 123, 126
  All Saints Church, 104
  Assembly Rooms, 45
  Assizes at, 40, 64
  George Inn, 43
  Riots at (1831), 64
Derbyshire
  County Infirmary, 66
  Deputy Lieutenants 30, 32, 37
  Justices of the Peace, 28, 30, 37, 53, 66
  Lords Lieutenant, 30
  Parliamentary representation, 40, 44, 64
  Sheriff, 30, 32, 34, 40–1, 44, 45, 53, 64, 68, 71, 75, 76, 117
  Volunteer Cavalry, see Yeomanry
  Yeomanry, 54, 64, 66, 117
Derby Hills, Derbys, 90, 94
Dethick, Dorothy, 31
Dewick, Petty, plasterer, 101
Devonshire, 5th Duke of, 54
Dickinson, Mrs., 49
Dimsdale, Dimminsdale, Derbys., 95
Dishley Grange Farm, Leics., 95
Doncaster, Yorks., races, 45
Donington, Leics.
  Park, 52, 106
  Stone, 99
Drakelow Hall, Derbys., 30, 51
Drayton Beauchamp, Bucks., 125
Drury-Lowe family, 88
Dudley, John, Earl of Warwick and Duke of Northumberland, 20

Eames, William, landscape-gardener, 121, 125
Eborall, Thomas, joiner, 108
Elizabeth I, Queen, 20
Enclosure, agricultural, 63, 94
Essex, Walter Devereux, 1st Earl of, 89
Etty, William, painter, 63
Exhibition, International (1862), 117

Fairbrother, Abraham, gamekeeper, 67
Farington, Joseph, 55
Faunt, Anthony, 33
Faunt, Barbara, 31. 33
Ferneley, John, painter, 62, 63, 68
Findern, Derbys., 24, 89, 94
Findern family, 24, 25, 31, 33, 89
Fitzherbert family, 90
Flash, Staffs., 62
Flight & Robson, musical instrument-makers, 117
Foremark, Derbys., 34, 90, 95, 96
Fossils, collection of, 70, 78

Gardner, Thomas, architect, 106–7
Gatton Park, Surrey, 50
Gell, Sir John, 32
Gibbs, James, architect, 103–4
Gilks, William, master-builder, 105
Gillow of Lancaster, furniture-maker, 111
Gillray, James, 55
Gilpin, Sawrey, painter, 47
Glossopdale, Derbys., 30
Glover, John, painter, 63
Glover, Stephen, topographer, 46
Gough, Sir Henry, Bart., 43
Goupy, Lewis, decorative painter, 125
Grace-Dieu, Leics., 20, 31, 33
Grand Tour, 43, 44, 48
Greaves, R. C., land-agent, 54, 94, 106
Greville, Hon. Charles, 54
Gresley, Catherine, 30, 31
Gresley, Thomas, 30
Grime, Thomas, land-agent, 95
Grimwood-Taylor, J. R. S., 76

Hanbury, R. W., M.P., 74
Hardwick Hall, Derbys., 98

HARPUR (see also Crewe)
  FAMILY
    archives, 8, 91
    arms, 33

    baronetcy, 33, 34, 88
    crest, 33, 105, 110
    estates, 96–7
    mottoes, 24, 36, 56
  INDIVIDUALS
    Harpur, Anne (Mrs. Borlase Warren), 36, 42
    Harpur, Lady Caroline (née Manners), 43, 44, 46, 125
    Harpur, Catherine, Lady (née Crewe), 37–9, 42, 56, 126
    Harpur, Catherine (Lady Gough), 39, 43
    Harpur, Charles (d.1770), 44
    Harpur, Edward (d.1761), 39, 43
    Harpur, Lady Frances (née Greville), 44, 45, 47, 48–50, 54, 58, 60, 66, 78, 115
    Harpur, George, see Crewe, Sir George
    Harpur, Sir Harry, see Harpur, Sir Henry, 6th Bart.
    Harpur, Henry (16th cent.), 21
    Harpur, Henry (17th cent.), 31
    Harpur, Henry (d.1793), 50
    Harpur, Sir Henry, 1st Bart. (d.1639), 20, 21, 32, 33, 34, 120
    Harpur, Sir Henry, 5th Bart. (d.1748), 38, 40, 42, 43, 115, 125
    Harpur, Sir Henry, 6th Bart. (d.1789), 44, 45, 47, 48, 91, 94, 106, 117, 121
    Harpur, Sir Henry, 7th Bart. (d.1819), see Crewe, Sir Henry
    Harpur, Jane (née Findern), 24, 25
    Harpur, Jemima (Lady Palmer), 43
    Harpur, John (d.1622), 31
    Harpur, John, of Breadsall (d.1622), 31
    Harpur, John, of Twyford, 34, 40
    Harpur, John (d.1780), 38, 43, 126
    Harpur, Sir John (d.1464), 21
    Harpur, Sir John (d.1622), 25, 28–31, 90
      monument to, 30, 31
    Harpur, Sir John (d.1679), 31, 32, 89
    Harpur, Sir John, 2nd Bart. (d.1669), 31, 34
    Harpur, Sir John, 3rd Bart. (d.1681), 31, 36
    Harpur, Sir John, 4th Bart. (d.1741), 36–42, 91, 92, 97, 98, 99, 104, 105, 115, 120
      monument to, 41, 42, 126
    Harpur, Louisa Matilda, 50
    Harpur, Mary (Lady Holte), 43
    Harpur, Nanny, Lady, see Crewe, Nanny
    Harpur, Richard (d.1577), 21–5, 89
      monument to, 21, 24, 25
    Harpur, Richard, of Littleover, 40
    Harpur, Sir Richard (d. 1619), 31
    Harpur, Sir Richard, of Littleover (d.1635), 25, 26, 31
    Harpur, Selina (Mrs. Lovell), 50, 70
    Harpur Crewe, Airmyne (d.1958), 72–3
    Harpur-Crewe, Airmyne Isabel Marie, 79
    Harpur Crewe, Alice (d.1920), 70
    Harpur-Crewe, Charles Arthur Richard (d.1981), 75–6, 78, 97, 117
    Harpur Crewe, Charles Hugh (d.1874), 50
    Harpur Crewe, Edmund Lewis (d.1874), 50, 72
    Harpur Crewe, Capt. Evelyn (d. 1877), 66
    Harpur Crewe, Georgiana, Lady (née Lovell), 65, 70, 111
    Harpur-Crewe, Henry Francis, 77, 79, 82, 83
    Harpur Crewe, Rev. Henry (d. 1883), 125
    Harpur Crewe, Hilda, see Mosley
    Harpur Crewe, Hugo (d.1905), 70, 74
    Harpur Crewe, Isabel, Lady (née Adderley), 71, 115
    Harpur Crewe, Sir John, 9th Bart.

Harpur Crewe, Sir John – *cont.*
  (d.1886), 67–70, 95, 111, 115, 117
  monument to, 126
Harpur Crewe, John Edmund
  (d.1903), 72
Harpur Crewe, Capt. Richard
  (d.1896), 66
Harpur Crewe, Richard Fynderne
  (d.1921), 68, 74, 75
Harpur Crewe, Sir Vauncey, 10th
  Bart. (d.1924), 7, 68, 70–4, 91,
  95, 96, 115, 117
  monument to, 126
Hastings family, 90, 95
Hawkins, Nanny, *see* Crewe, Nanny
Haydn, Josef, 53, 54
Hemington, Leics., 74, 89, 90, 94
Henry I, King, 15
Henry II, King, 15
Hewitt, Thomas, 101
Hinton, Northants., 47
Historic Buildings Council, 82
Holt, Simon, mason, 101
Holte, Sir Lester, 43
Hopton stone, 125
Horses, horse racing, 45, 47
Howard, Hon. Henry, 31
Huet, —, 101, 103
Huitt, Mr., 101
Huntingdon, 5th Earl of, 30
Huntingdon, Selina, Countess of, 48

Ingleby, Derbys., 54, 106

Jenney, Airmyne, *see* Harpur-Crewe,
  Airmyne Isabel Marie
Jenney, Arthur, 75
Jenney, Charles, *see* Harpur-Crewe,
  Charles (d.1981)
Jenney, Frances, 75
Jenney, Henry Francis, *see*
  Harpur-Crewe, Henry Francis
Jordan, John, mason, 101
Johnson, William, surveyor, 101

Kedleston, Derbys, 68, 88
Kendall family, 89
Kettle, Tilly, painter, 78, 113
Kingsey, Bucks., painting of, 23
Kirkland, Thomas, 91

Lamerie, Paul de, silversmith, 37
Landseer, Sir Edwin, painter, 63
Lausanne, Switzerland, 48
Lawrence, Sir Thomas, painter, 47
Lawson, Nigel, 83
Lead, marketing of, 20, 95
Ledoux, Claude Nicolas, architect, 109
Leech, John, carpenter, 101
Lepidoptera, collection of, 71, 72
Levinge, Sir Richard, 40
Lichfield, Staffs., 36
  Bishop of, 17
  Races, 45
Line, lime-works, 88, 89, 95, 121, 122
Linnell, John, painter, 23, 63
Littleover, Derbys., 28, 40, 41
Locko, Derbys, 88
London, George, gardener, 37, 123
London
  Barnard's Inn, 21

Fleet Prison, 29
Inner Temple, 21, 83
Park Street, no. 35, 50
Residence in, 37–9
St. James's Place, no. 26, 42, 44
Stevens's Auction Rooms, 71
Tower of, 20
Upper Grosvenor Street, no. 35, 44,
  47, 50
Long Alders, 123
Longnor, Staffs., 63, 94
l'Orme, Philibert de, architect, 102, 103
Lovell, Genl. Sir Lovell Benjamin
  (Badcock), 65
Lovell, Vice-Adml. William Stanhope
  (Badcock), 65, 70
Luffenham, Rutland, 42

Manners, Lady Caroline, *see* Harpur,
  Lady Caroline
May Place, Kent, 50
Melbourne, Derbys., 68, 97
  Hall, 38, 40, 88, 90
Melville, Rodney, architect, 111
Mereworth Castle, Kent, 50
Middleton, 2nd Lord, 44
Milton, Derbys., 89, 94
Minerals, collection of, 70, 78, 117
Mines, 95
Moira, Earl of, 52, 106
Moore, Dr. John, 34
Moravian sect, 48
Mosley, Col. Godfrey, 23, 74, 111
Mosley, Hilda, 74, 75, 78, 96, 97
Mosley, Rev. Rowland, 74
Müller, W. J., artist, 63
Music, musicians, 30, 34, 36, 44, 54, 117

Naples, paintings of, 23, 63
National Heritage Memorial Fund, 82,
  83
National Trust, 7, 8, 82, 83, 85, 97, 117
Newton Solney, Derbys., 15, 90
Norton, 1st Lord, 68
Nottingham, 43, 78. 96, 101

Old Parks, Leics., 91
Orange, Prince of, 46
Ornithology, 70–1
Osmaston Hall, Derbys., 64, 88
Ossington Hall, Notts., 109
Outram, Benjamin, civil engineer, 96
Oxford
  Bodleian Library, 85
  Brasenose College, 25, 33, 43
  Christ Church, 44
  Queen's College, 36

Paintings, collection of, 63, 68
Palmer, Frances, 31
Palmer, Sir Thomas, Bart., 43
Parliamentary elections, 40, 44, 64
Peak Park, 97
Pegg, Agathos, gamekeeper, 71, 72, 73
Phillips, H. W., painter, 85
Phillips, Sir Richard, 61
Pierrepont, Sir George, 30
Pierrepont, Isabella, 30, 31
Pilkington, Francis, composer, 34
Pistern Hill, Derbys, 95, 99
Pokers Leys, 123
Port, Elizabeth, 24, 25

Port, Sir John (d.1541), 24, 25
Port, Sir John (d.1557), 24, 25, 89
Potlock, Derbys., 89
Portland sheep, 47, 68, 126
Prest or Priest, John, 17, 95
Price, Francis, carpenter, 106
Putney Park, Surrey, 47
Pye, Richard, 40

Quarnford, Staffs., 62

Reading, —, house-painter, 101
Reinagle, R. R., painter, 60
Repton, Derbys., 89, 90, 94, 96
  Park, 52, 72, 90
  Priory, 16–17, 95
  School, 24–5, 50, 76, 106
Reresby, Mary, 31
Reservoir, 78, 118, 122
Ricciardelli, Gabriele, painter, 23, 53
Richmond, Yorks., races, 45
Roiley family, carvers, 24
Rugby School, Warwicks., 58, 67
Rushall, Staffs., 21
Rutland, 2nd Duke of, 43

Sampson, William, dramatist, 30
Sartorius, Francis (?), horse-painter, 47
SAVE, 82, 83
Sawley, Derbys., 28
Sedley, Sir Charles, 47
Servants, 74
Settlements, strict, 78, 86, 88
Shaw, John, land-agent, 95
Shirley, Sir Henry, Bart., 34
Shrewsbury, Elizabeth, Countess of, 28
Shrewsbury, George Talbot, 6th Earl
  of, 28
Shrewsbury, Gilbert Talbot, 7th Earl of,
  28, 30
Shudi, Burkat, harpsichord-maker, 117
Silver, 37, 45, 117
Sinfin, Derbys., 89, 96
Smisby, Derbys., 15, 36, 89, 95, 99
Smith, Francis, master-mason, 104
Smith, John Raphael, painter, 44
Smith, John (Warwick), painter, 47
Smith, William, land-agent, 95
Smith & Sharp, silversmiths, 45
Southwood, Leics., 90, 91, 96
Spencer, 2nd Earl, 47
Staffordshire, Harpur estate in, 61–3,
  89, 91, 94, 95, 97
Stanhope family, 102
Stanhope, 4th Earl, 17
Stanhope, Thomas, 40
Stanton-by-Bridge, Derbys., 24, 68, 89,
  94
Staunton Harold, Leics., 34, 91
Steen, Jan, painter, 63
Stevens, Henry Isaac, architect, 109, 110
Stenson, Derbys., 96
Stone House, Kent, 50
Stourfield House, Hants., 50
Suffolk, 1st Earl of, 31
Swarkeston, Derbys., 68, 90, 96
  Banqueting House, 29, 30
  Bowling Green, 30
  Bridge, 30
  Battle of, 32
  Casino, 51, 52

  Church, 21, 24, 25, 30
  Harpur Estate, 24, 33, 36, 89
  House, 24, 30, 33, 98, 99
  Swarkeston Lows Farm, 95

Tadworth Court, Surrey, 47
Tamworth, Staffs., 44
Tatham & Bailey, furniture-makers,
  109, 111
Tatshall Fee, Derbys., 90
Taxal, Cheshire, 49
Taylor, Sir Robert, architect, 106
Taylor, Sarah, lady's maid, 66
Taylor, Simpson & Mosley, solicitors,
  74
Thacker, Thomas, 17–18
Thomas, Lieut., R. S., painter, 65
Ticknall, Derbys., 34, 66, 68, 74, 89, 90,
  96, 97, 120, 122
  Church, 109
  Coalmine, 95
  Enclosure, 94
  Estate Office, 95
  Limeworks, 96
  Manor, 15, 90
  Pottery, 19, 117
Tomson, Clifton, horse-painter, 54
Toys, 77, 81, 117
Trafalgar, Battle of, 65, 78
Tramway, industrial, 86, 95–6
Trent, river, 30
  Bronze Age Swords, 117
  Fisheries, 91, 96
  Navigation, 96
Twyford, Derbys., 24, 36, 89

Uniforms, military, 78, 117

Vawser, G. R., artist, 121

Walker, Anne, lady's maid, 66
Walton-on-Trent, Derbys., 15
Ward, James, painter, 63
Warslow, Staffs., 62, 68, 70
  Dale Mine, 95
Warwick, 1st Earl of, 44, 47
Wedgwood tiles, 125
Wendsley or Wennesley, Richard, 20, 98
West, Susan, 31
Westminster School, 43
Whelpdale, —, carpenter, 101
Whittaker family, 58
Wilden (Wilne) Ferry, Derbys., 96
Wilkins, William, sr., architect, 52,
  106–9, 122
Wilkinson, Sir Gardner, 85, 111, 121
Williams, Samuel, footman, 66
Williamson, Sir Joseph, 36
Williamson, Nicholas, 28
Willington, Derbys., 89, 90, 94
  Grange, 23, 111
Willoughby, Anne, 31, 36
Willoughby, Frances, 32, 36
Willoughby of Parham, Lord, 31, 36
Wilmot, Sir Robert, Bart., 54
Wilmot-Horton, Sir Robert, 64
Wilmot-Horton family, 88
Wise, Henry, gardener, 37, 123
Witt, Rev. Matthew, 57
Woburn Abbey, Beds., 95
Woolley, William, 42
Worcester, 44
Wright, —, carver, 101